59

LESSONS

59 LESSONS

WORKING WITH THE WORLD'S ELITE COACHES, ATHLETES & SPECIAL FORCES

FERGUS CONNOLLY

Ordering Information:
Quantity sales. Special discounts are available on quantity
purchases by corporations, associations, and others.
For details, contact the publisher at
info@fergusconnolly.com

ISBN: 978-0-9600509-0-1

Library of Congress Control Number: 2018913956

PCIP: Pending

Book cover and layout design by *the*BookDesigners

Printed in the United States of America

To all those who selflessly gave their time
to help me on my journey so far.

"We are like dwarfs sitting on the shoulders of giants. We see more, and things that are more distant, than they did, not because our sight is superior or because we are taller than they, but because they raise us up, and by their great stature add to ours."

JOHN OF SALISBURY, THE METALOGICON, 1159

CONTENTS

FOREWORD

Over the course of my 22-year career as a US Navy SEAL, I learned hundreds of tough lessons the hard way. It was only after a galvanizing event that I typically recognized the true value of a concept, theory, or technique. Not until the latter stages of my operational career did I have the understanding I needed to start keeping a journal, in which I recorded the most critical thoughts and lessons learned from my experiences in combat. To do so with clarity, I created a daily routine that would allow me to quiet my mind and shift into a state of deep reflection before I needed to perform.

The helicopter ride during the infiltration phase of approaching an enemy target was something that I always looked forward to. This started the countdown for my deliberate, pre-performance routine. On our way to a target site and while infiltrating the enemy in the darkness of night, our preferred mode of transportation was always a helicopter. There was a blackness in the sky that I found calming and quiet. The only audible sound was the rhythmic, hypnotic pulsing of the rotors above our heads.

I loved these rides not because a helicopter was the quickest or most convenient method of transit – which it certainly was – but rather because these journeys were meditative. While flying, I'd access a zone of balanced juxtaposition – calm and amped. This state of mental clarity was so precise that everything else in the world ceased to exist. So much so that when I stepped into the chaos of combat, I was highly situationally aware, assertive, poised, and precise.

The process began the moment that our assault team finished its general briefing. This almost always took place standing around a fire pit in full gear, using nothing more than an unglamorous map, a standard dry-erase board, and a marker. Immediately after the briefing, we'd load a military version of a school bus, a bread truck with an empty cargo space we could pile into, or a convoy of overloaded pickup trucks, and make our way to the airfield. It was at this point that the silence and stillness started. For the uninitiated, it could overwhelm you if your mind wasn't strong enough to handle the pressure of what was at stake. Yet it was at this exact moment that the next phase of my mental routine would begin. I'd mindfully absorb the heaviness of the night and silently appreciate the character and capability of the warriors that embodied my SEAL family.

Immediately after the bus ride, my focus deepened. As I walked alongside my teammates toward the flight line, I would consciously focus on the temporal environment, which was usually only one of two extremes: bitter, nail biting, numb-your-face cold, or relentless, sweltering heat that felt like being in a convection oven. The places we operated in have no other seasons. The cold seductively tempted us to slow down and stop moving, while the heat was so thick and merciless that it punished us from sunrise to sunset. During this time, I would accept mother nature's extremes, let the air soak into my skin, throat, and lungs, and feel the elements invigorating my blood. Flying through the vast, all-enveloping darkness, my focus sharpened.

When approaching the helicopter just before stepping onto the ramp, the orange glow from the roaring twin turbines just below the main rotor would send a gust of heat across my face and neck. I'd use this as a cue to look up at the sky through my NVGs (night vision goggles) and notice the illumination from thousands of stars in the immense sky above. In this micro-moment, I created space to remind myself that the rest of the world was bigger than the evil, harsh, and unforgiving reality I was about to confront. I needed to protect my mind, remind myself that the world is a beautiful place, and resolve that the ugliness of the enemy and their total disregard for human life would not impact my willingness to persevere. I refused to let them affect my assuredness, and decided to never surrender my belief in the inherent goodness of the people I loved or the God I trusted.

My favorite place to sit was always at the rear of the aircraft facing the tail, which would often be left open for our entire ride to the objective. I'd purposely load last and seek out this spot so that I could observe the landscape below, as it always placed me into a state of awe. Over the duration of my career as a SEAL, I saw a multitude of countries, ethnicities, and historical sites. But there is nothing quite like the terrain of the Middle East and seeing it from a helicopter was a truly unique experience.

While in flight, I would shift my attention away from the demands of the event that would soon take place, and instead think about all the people who loved and supported me, and just how badly I wished that they could view this scene through my eyes, if only for a minute. How incredibly overwhelmed they would be if they could see how close we flew next to vast mountain ranges, and if they could sense the impossible weightlessness of the helicopter as it peeled around cliff faces. I smiled while thinking about how they'd react if they could watch as we suddenly dropped hundreds of feet in the air, screaming straight into ravines at full speed and getting so close to the canyon floor that I could see small rocks and smell blades of grass. Only to launch out again a few seconds later into huge expanses of uninterrupted desert, all the while evading detection by using speed and skill to our advantage.

This would inevitably prompt me to humbly realize how much I owed to all those who made it possible for me to carry such an incredible amount of responsibility, and to have the greatest job in the world: a Navy SEAL.

At this point, maybe you're wondering, "How could it be that a SEAL, on the way into a complex and volatile environment, would allow their focus to be on anything other than the mission and his survival?" Or perhaps you're thinking, "Wouldn't it be more prudent to use that time to mentally rehearse each step of the operation and analyze all the things that needed to happen if something went wrong?" These are great and relevant questions, and my answer is a simple and succinct phrase: "The check is already in the mail."

By the time we got on the helicopter, the deed was done. We'd put in the work already. We knew our purpose. We trusted each other with our lives to be in the right place at the right time under these circumstances. All the studying, training, and rehearsing up to this point had prepared us for those moments. Well before the insert, I had read every post-operation report that I could get my hands on from previous deployments and searched for any lesson learned that could give me an advantage. I made it a point to obsessively study the older, more experienced operators around me and listen intently to them in the hope of absorbing their wisdom. I made sure to evaluate their tactical decision making in training to improve my capacity to lead when given the chance. I would never lose an opportunity to ask a senior SEAL for their assessment when I was lost or lacked perspective and, surprisingly, the answers to my questions challenged me more than any other aspect of my training.

The time to prepare for the operation was yesterday. During the transit to the target, the things I needed most were stillness and peace, with a few subtle cues to remind me of my larger purpose. This approach enabled everything from my studying and training to materialize at the highest level of performance. Without my routine, I would unconsciously drift into a state of over-analysis, needlessly scrutinizing the details of the operation until the moment we reached the target area. That was, at least in my opinion, pointless. It'd be about as smart as pulling an all-night cramming session before a big exam, rather than getting a full night's sleep and showing up for the test fresh, alert, and focused. Sure, it can get the job done, but it's not how a professional practitioner operates.

I wouldn't be honest if I said I had practiced my helicopter routine religiously throughout my entire career. I wish I had. Instead, I made my share of mistakes on and off the battlefield, and I learned tough lessons the hard way. It took years for me to even accept that a pre-performance routine was important, and then many more to shape and perfect my own one. In doing so, I employed one of the most critical lessons I've ever learned: always use your environment to your advantage to gain an edge over your opponent. In the illustration that I just shared, the opponent was my mind, and the real battle was navigating past my tendency to wander toward negativity, which would've allowed doubt to overrun my thoughts.

Looking into the rearview mirror at my career and assessing all it took to refine my skillsets, I'm astounded at the long list of lessons that helped sharpen my craft. The most valuable ones that defined my personal and professional success – those that revealed my ability to recover from near total disaster or to operate under high levels of duress – were acquired in a piece-meal manner. I collected them over the course of more than two decades through earned successes, miserable failures, and stories told around a campfire or while having a few beers with my teammates. What I didn't have to help me was a one-stop performance bible that contained all the wisdom I was taught and surrounded by. There was never anything that consolidated every piece of imperative information into a single, highly applicable field manual.

59 Lessons is that book.

What you're reading is a carefully organized, expertly expressed catalogue. Fergus obtained the knowledge conveyed here by dedicating his entire adult life to studying the most competitive arenas in the world, and then putting what he learned into practice. These lessons are relatable to anyone who is looking for a competitive edge in their own context. What you have in your hands is an incredible opportunity to gain ground on your battlefield. Use this book to sharpen your leadership and learn the mental skills that will enhance your life in every way.

I urge you to relentlessly attack the content in these pages so you can create positive change. Gather the parts and pieces that will help you get to where you need to be. Your mission is to turn this book into your journal. So grab a highlighter and illuminate the themes that resonate with you. Keep a pencil close by and use arrows, lines, and circles to connect the words and concepts. Allow Fergus to create a dialogue that will enable you to build a strategy and win your battles.

It's time for you to perform at the highest level, to separate yourself from the herd, and step boldly into excellence. Be relentless.

BEN IVES
US NAVY SEAL (RETIRED)

INTRODUCTION

I've never been someone to think like or follow the herd. This has made for an unplanned and certainly interesting career. I've been fortunate to learn from many great people all over the world, some of whom you've almost certainly heard of, and many more who you haven't, but can benefit from.

Sports, conflict, and business are not life, they are all subsets of life. There are many lessons we can all learn from each to help us with the challenges we face in our own world. By committing my career lessons to print, I hope that they can be passed on and the influence of these teachers preserved.

Though I have always had a passion for helping others, this book allows me to demonstrate we're simply standing on the shoulders of giants.

Enjoy the lessons I've learned on my journey. I hope they help you on yours!

Fergus

NOTE

In this mutable world, there has been a change in how conflicts are fought. This has led to increased attention drawn to the quiet professionals of the Special Operations community.

Names are either changed or purposely blacked out, not just for the security of the operator or their unit, but, more importantly, out of respect for the true ethos of their profession.

In order not to reveal too much, I use the universal title of "commander" to identify those in leadership and "operator" for the soldiers, marines, sailors, and their performance staff who have taught me so much.

The lessons for the reader are preserved and written to remain relevant and accurate.

Finally, many of the lessons here are from my experience in mostly male sports. This is for no reason other than the fact that I've almost exclusively worked in such environments due to circumstance, not conscious choice. That said, the lessons in this book apply across all domains, genders, and ages.

THE JOURNEY

To say that my path into sports performance is unusual is an understatement. My parents moved back to Ireland from the US the year before I was born so my father could take a new teaching position. Growing up in the 1980s in Ireland, I was fascinated by sports from the moment my father lifted me over the turnstiles to watch Gaelic football games on a Sunday with him.

I started playing Gaelic football (Ireland's national sport) at age 16, which made me a latecomer. I grew up in a very special part of Ireland called Scotstown, not far from the border between Southern and Northern Ireland. Playing at the local club, I had some wonderful examples of leadership from the outset. To catch up with the rest of the boys my age, I did the only thing I knew to improve, which was listen to the older players and work hard. This meant reading and studying the greats of the game to try and uncover the secrets to their success.

I read newspaper and magazine articles about leaders, athletes, and all kinds of training. I lifted weights, ran hills with a backpack with half a concrete block in it. When I felt like I lacked endurance late in games, added in long road mountain runs. Sometimes if I thought my speed was lacking, I'd do more weight training and more hill work. If I ever got injured – straining a muscle, for example – I'd learn everything I could about rehabbing it. I'd study flexibility training to try and prevent a recurrence in the future. I just used the information I had available to me. Whatever it takes.

EDUCATION OF A GENERALIST

I was younger in school than most of my peers, starting at the University of Limerick and finishing my first year before I turned 18. When I arrived on campus, I was like a child in a candy store. Remember, these were in the years before the lightning-fast internet connections we've come to take for granted. Being a voracious reader, I was delighted with the large collection of sports science and physiology books available in the university library. At that point, there weren't really careers in sports science – and certainly none in Ireland – but I was still fascinated by this future possibility.

I finished my four-year teaching degree in materials, construction, and technology just before my 21st birthday and decided to stay on and do a master's in advanced manufacturing technology. Teaching had taught me the importance of planning, human learning, personal interaction, and how to manage groups.

My master's degree was very different, familiarizing me with a lot of technology and design concepts. I learned about the human-machine interface, the value of ergonomics, and was introduced to concepts like just-in-time, quality control, scheduling, and planning.

That led me to completing my PhD in computer optimization, which taught me a lot about advanced programming and the unforgiving nature of coding, as well as the importance and value of research. I also developed the mindset needed to complete a demanding academic project independently.

All of these dissimilar degrees provided a skillset that I have carried with me to this day. No education is ever wasted. My experience in the world of business and manufacturing always makes it easier to explain military or sporting performances to commanders and company executives in their terms. Most importantly, my formal education provided me with models of thinking that helped me approach problem solving with a completely different perspective.

APPRENTICESHIP

When I had breaks in my studies, I'd feed my real passion by connecting with coaches in different parts of Ireland and asking to come visit them. Later when I saved a bit more money, I started to go further afield and traveled to Canada, the US, New Zealand, Australia, and anywhere I could to learn on the front lines. I had a zeal for understanding all aspects of human performance and a hunger for discovery.

This book is essentially a story of apprenticeship with some of the greatest coaches, players, and teams in the sports world. These are lessons they taught me about winning in business, military, and sports.

My on-the-job apprenticeship gave me a solid foundation for my own career journey, which began when I became the first full-time sports scientist in the Premier League with Bolton Wanderers. From there I have made many different stops in full-time, part-time, and consulting roles at the college, pro, and national team level in every major field and court sport.

This has given me the opportunity to immerse myself in the unique culture of Munster, Harlequins, St. Frances

Academy, Cricket Australia, and Northampton Saints, witness the significance of maintaining a small backroom staff at Blackburn Rovers, the Cleveland Browns, and Liverpool, and see the optimal application of strength and conditioning with the Atlanta Falcons and San Francisco 49ers. I've also been privileged to work with some of the world's greatest boxers and athletes at the Welsh national rugby union team, University of Michigan football, and much more.

To work alongside so many of the greats has not only been a blessing, but also allows me to pass on their lessons to others in the sports, military, and corporate world. With every organization, I've given my all and worked ceaselessly to serve, and now I share those lessons with teams and corporations around the world.

WINNING
HABITS

NEVER BRING A GUN TO A GUN FIGHT

1

In business and sports, you need to be ruthless in your focus to win, but careful in how you achieve it.

Bill Sweetenham is arguably the most successful swim coach of all time. Like many of the greats, he is a master storyteller. One year just before the Olympics, he brought some of the British team members to Ireland to train. One of Bill's female swimmers was complaining that she was homesick and missed her dog. Soccer hardman Roy Keane was ironically doing a campaign for guide dogs at the time. Bill "borrowed" a large cut-out of Roy standing next to a dog and brought it to practice the next day. He handed the girl a water pistol and said, "Just how hard do you want to win? Right, here's a gun. It's shoot the dog or win an Olympic gold medal, which one?"

The poor girl froze in shock.

"Too late," Bill continued. "The dog should've been dead by now."

Not surprisingly, when news of this leaked out, it got attention. The RSPCA picketed his house and he got truckloads of hate mail, not that it seemed to bother Bill in the slightest. Of course, though extreme, his point was: either you're dedicated to winning or you're not. And if you are, it's going to require ruthlessness.

Winning and wanting to win doesn't make you a bad person. In fact, it's more admirable that one would want to be successful – at whatever they attempt to do. How you respond to winning or losing is the key, but more on that later.

A senior Special Forces commander reminded me often that you need to have "an iron fist in a velvet glove." Several coaches I've encountered over the years have exemplified this need to be gentle, but firm, kind, but brutally clear, and compassionate, yet ruthless. By the time my colleague Craig White brought Bill Sweetenham to talk to the Welsh rugby team, he had masterminded the unprecedented success of the Australian swimming team. He then went on to do the same for Britain's Olympic swimming program.

Bill was the most ruthless coach I've ever encountered – and that's a compliment. Up until then I'd never really appreciated the benefits of ruthlessness. If there was a picture alongside the definition of "winning" in the dictionary, there'd be a photo of Bill. I respect the desire to succeed second only to how one acts after they win or lose. The bravery to give everything to something exposes a vulnerability that is most admirable.

"BE COMPASSIONATELY RUTHLESS."

Bill demonstrated to me that you have to be very clear about your intention to win, and then commit everything to it. Many who've heard Bill speak will recall hearing him tell the harrowing story of how he was kicked out of his home at an early age and had to become self-sufficient and tough to not only survive, but also learn the coaching craft. He expected similar toughness and resilience from his swimmers, and though he'd listen to explanations, he would not suffer excuses. Until then I'd never really understood the clarity of ruthlessness. It was like a weight had been lifted off my shoulders.

In Bill's world, winning was not a participation sport. It was only for the few who were willing to make it a precedence. He looked after his athletes and staff, but he also believed that telling them hard truths was vital. Nathan Buckley, John McCloskey, Rodney Eade, Carlos Queiroz, Mick O'Dwyer, Mick Malthouse, and the Australian football coach Alastair Clarkson, who I'd pester at every chance, had similar mindsets that echoed the words of British Cycling mastermind Dave Brailsford, who coined the term "be compassionately ruthless."

The other lesson I learned from many in the Special Operations community is that it's never over until you're at home smoking a cigar on your porch. In other words, destroy the opposition completely and never give up, no matter what the score is until you're in the locker room victorious. Think you've won before that and you usually trip up before the finish line. If anything, bring more than enough force to win. Never bring just a gun to a gun fight – bring everything to overpower your opponent.

This means that you must prepare for every single possibility in the game scenario. Sir Clive Woodward also exemplified this. Though he never lost sight of his teams' ultimate goals, Sir Clive had an incredible attention to detail and never left anything to chance. When he came into the England setup, he brought in the best people in every area, from his assistant coaches to consultants to the team chef. Yes, the best talent costs more, but he knew it was necessary to get results on the biggest stage – a belief that proved to be well founded given all that the team achieved. The cost of losing was potentially much bigger than the expense of winning.

Have you counted the costs and are you willing to pay the price?

COROLLARY

Occasionally leaders get focused on the end to the degree that they pursue it blindly. They forget that this is a people business. Many coaches in today's world border on being sociopathic. While this brings short-term success, in the medium or long-term, it ends in failure and loss of any respect. Find the balance between ruthlessness and people management. It's not what you do, it's how you do it.

APPLICATION

In business or sports, the best coaches are clear about their goals. Everyone on your team must know the goal and be aware of the end game. Be clear, be direct. Say it as you see it. Jack Welch calls this "candor." You may hurt feelings initially and be disliked temporarily. In the long run you will be respected by your organization and opponent alike.

"Captain and coach must be seen to be banging the same drum."

— SIR CLIVE WOODWARD

THE AIM IS NOT TO WIN ONCE

2

Do not plan to win one championship, but to win many. Legacies are built on sustained success.

When I first met Alastair Clarkson, I was a green rookie just starting my first full-time job as a sports scientist and assistant strength coach at Bolton Wanderers football club. He was just starting his coaching career. It was early in the Premier League season and Alastair was visiting for a week to learn what he could from other sports. Our paths have crossed many times since. "Clarko" had a rare quality that I recognized in a few special coaches like Bill Sweetenham, Alex Ferguson, Jim Gavin, and Pat Howard – a desire to utterly dominate for multiple seasons, not just one game.

It's a combination of hunger and strategy that is surprisingly rare. An ability to plan with what is referred to in conflict as "the long war." Many leaders get caught up in focusing on what's right in front of them, without preserving their focus on the big picture. You will observe this often in teams who win a big game with great purpose, but stumble against lesser opponents or can't put together back-to-back winning seasons.

Many of the best leaders focus on building an organization and team that relentlessly dominates with resilience. The rugby league coach Wayne Bennett was probably my best teacher on this point. He might well lose occasionally, but the long-term goal and attitude remains intact. Recognizing this quality changed my perspective completely.

My goal has always been to help build an organization/team that dominates its sport so completely and relentlessly that the governing body has to change a rule to stop us. To get to this level, you need a plan that establishes a defined path to consistent excellence:

- Rather than saying, "We will win every game," it focuses on long-term performance
- It directly identifies the need for a roster and pathway of developing players to continue it
- It creates an ideal greater than just a coach or player that everyone in the organization could identify with and contribute to
- It doesn't change in the face of defeat
- It personalizes the goal to the people in the organization in a way that makes it become apparent the only real competitor was ourselves

Such a conscious approach to cultivating dominance was the most striking thing I saw in Bill Walsh's players at the 49ers. Keena Turner was an all-time great linebacker, but I think he has nightmares from my time in San Francisco. I would pester Keena with questions about how Bill coached and how Eddie DeBartolo ran the team. Keena, Guy McIntyre, and others spoke about Walsh and DeBartolo with a sense of reverence and awe. But the theme that always came through was constant focus on their goal for perfection in performance.

To be truly great like that 49ers team, you need to concentrate on continual improvement every day. If you fixate on a single win alone, there is often a false sense of completion when the real work is only just beginning. You can't ignore immediate challenges, but must preserve a long-term mindset.

"BUILD A LEGACY FROM THE BEGINNING."

Walsh was empowered to succeed and help his players excel because the team owner, Eddie DeBartolo, was so supportive. If you're serious about building a dynasty and dominating over a long period of time, you must look after your people from the top down and the bottom up. The best example of this today (outside of the All Blacks) is Bob Kraft and Bill Belichick at the New England Patriots. Recognizing this, Tom Brady and other star players have been willing to take less than they're worth in the open market to stay and help the entire organization make something with an even greater, lasting impact: history. It's not about getting a win. It's about domination.

When I first met with Jim Gavin, the Dublin Gaelic football manager, we discussed winning an All-Ireland, but I made it clear that I felt we had to focus on building a dynasty by winning multiple championships. This meant doing things like creating a pathway for youth players, cultivating a longer-term view for senior ones, developing a game model, and maintaining staff continuity. The reason for this was that almost every team I'd seen win one national title never won the next one, largely because they hadn't had their eyes on creating a dynasty, but instead pursued a "win now" philosophy.

Three days after claiming the first All-Ireland trophy, Jim and I sat together in a quiet corner of The Gibson Hotel formulating a plan to win the following year's championship. Continued excellence must always be the goal for great teams.

What success are you striving toward that cannot be sustained without strategy?

COROLLARY

I once heard David Moyes, former Everton and Manchester United manager, being asked what the most important thing was for a young coach to do. He replied, "survive." In other words, if you don't win in the short-term, you will never reach your long-term goals. Have a long-term vision, but don't get too distracted by it. You must certainly win the immediate battle. Far too often, people have lofty dreams, but get distracted. Keep a balance. Know where you are starting from, be realistic about next steps, and keep your destination in mind.

APPLICATION

Decide what your immediate and short-term goals are. Choose the best approach to achieve them and hold nothing back. But after every decision is made, consider your long-term vision and how it impacts the long-term plan. If the "now" choice will negatively affect the "later" outcome, then adjust it. Find the immediate tactic that best fits the long-term strategy.

"Power isn't just about going forward. It's about not letting anything hold you back."

— PATRICK WILLIS

WE ONLY PLAY AWAY GAMES

3

Tell yourself you are the best in the world before going to bed. But in the morning, wake up and work like you're second best.

I was sitting across the desk from a Special Forces officer as the summer sun lit up his unassuming office. For the next hour, we shared lessons and philosophy on the selection and preparation of elite performers. This commander was responsible for the selection process of an elite Special Operations group.

"You can't compare what our players do to what your operators do," I said. "It's not the same at all. There are two special distinctions. First, we know when our games are and can plan training for them so we can be prepared. You can't schedule contact with the enemy. Second, if one of our guys makes a mistake, we 'get Monday.' We get to practice again and fix it. In your world, you don't."

"There's one other difference, Fergus," the commander replied calmly. "We only play away games."

The single biggest threat to successful teams is complacency. This can creep up in many forms. Sometimes it's media-induced "rat poison," as Nick Saban referred to it. It can also come from lack of focus or external distractions.

I've never forgotten the phrase, "We only play away games." It is a reminder that until the final whistle blows, you can never allow complacency to set in.

"COMPLACENCY KILLS."

It has been proven true again and again. On one occasion, I stayed at a hotel the night before a game and found schedules and training notes for another team who had stayed there the week before. We've all heard stories of game plans going suspiciously "missing" in hotels, too. It got me thinking about how easily complacency can take root and the sloppiness that results. Imagine if we'd been playing that team later in the season. We'd have had their entire game plan because someone wasn't paying attention to the details. Competition is difficult enough, without giving your opponent an undue edge.

Another officer who was responsible for selection at a similar elite Special Forces group told me how he was once called by the head of the overall unit. Out of 207 recruits who began one year, only seven were selected, a lower acceptance rate than the previous year, when 15 out of 240 trainees had made it through. The commander was asked to explain why so few had been accepted this time around. The officer responsible calmly explained that the men simply hadn't reached the required standard. He recognized that having fewer men would stretch the unit's capability. After hearing this explanation, the commander thanked the officer for not letting standards drop.

Complacency kills.

Treat everything like an away game.

You can't keep your foot on the gas while constantly glancing in the rearview mirror.

COROLLARY

Confidence is essential. Don't encourage fear, which is debilitating and self-destructive. When you have confidence with an absence of complacency, you end up with a healthy state of awareness in both your team and staff.

APPLICATION

Have fun and believe in your ability. Tease and joke about it, but never to the extent that it becomes a posture of over-confidence and arrogance. Humor is an excellent way to maintain this balance. Be great and know it, but keep an awareness and respect for the enemy and never get complacent. Remember that the enemy always gets a vote.

"It's football. Players move on, coaches move on. You got to roll with the punches."

— JUSTIN SMITH

ONLY THOSE WHO ENDURE

4

It is not those who can inflict the most, but those that can suffer the most who will conquer.

I've worked with many great teams, but when I was asked to consult with Munster Rugby a number of years ago it was as much an honor as a job. While people often put the All Blacks on a pedestal (and rightly so), Munster's culture is just as unique. At that time, they had several living legends of the international game playing for them. John Hayes, Doug Howlett, Ronan O'Gara, Paul O'Connell, Peter Stringer, Donncha O'Callaghan, and BJ Botha were all leaders. Keith Earls, Conor Murray, Peter O'Mahony, and a young Simon Zebo were all coming through. Tony McGahan was the head coach, having replaced Declan Kidney when he took over at Ireland. Next came Rob Penney, who in turn was followed by an Irish and Munster legend himself, Anthony "Axel" Foley.

O'Connell, O'Gara, O'Callaghan, Stringer, Howlett, and Hayes were all in their 30s and we implemented what became known as "The Maldini Project" to prolong their careers. All players had exceptional leadership qualities, but also invaluable experience. While the trend was to focus on training more and harder, head of strength and conditioning Bryce Cavanagh and I knew we had to allow these players to optimize and exploit the greatest advantage they had – their experience – while maintaining their physical ability.

The Maldini Project was named after Paolo Maldini, a product of the Milan Lab, who made his first team debut for AC Milan as a 16-year-old in 1985. He played his last game as a 41-year-old on May 31st, 2009. Maldini typified the message Bryce and I were trying to sell to the Munster players because Maldini optimized his biggest asset – tactical and technical experience – to play at a high level for 25 seasons, all at the same Serie A club. Legend has it that Maldini went through many games out-playing much younger opponents without having to make a single tackle by reading the game and being in the right place at the right time. The Munster players immediately recognized the message. The accompanying manual that we produced was player-focused and included sections on recovery, lifestyle, regeneration, and restoration. This was about doing things better, not doing more. Work hard on the field and then recover better off it.

We put one final message in the back of the book, and perhaps the most important of all. It came from a quote by Irish politician Terence MacSwiney. He was elected as Lord Mayor of Cork during the Irish War of Independence in 1920 and arrested by the British Army on charges of sedition. While incarcerated in Brixton Prison, he went on a hunger strike to protest what he saw as his unjust arrest. After 74 days, he died in October 1920. Though MacSwiney passed away, Ireland was changed forever by the conflict and the Irish Free State was created in 1922. The inscription at the back of the book read:

"It is not those who can inflict the most, but those that can suffer the most who will conquer."

The message was subtle. This was not all about recovery and rest, but about being smart in how the Munster players worked. They needed to bounce back better than anyone else so they could tolerate more suffering than any opponent. The subtext was that we would be fresher both mentally and physically, so we could endure the best our opposition could throw at us and, in turn, pressure them into mistakes. At the highest level in the final minutes of any tight game or in finals and playoffs, it's not the team who makes the biggest plays that prevails, but the one that makes the least errors. Anyone can inflict pain, but those who can endure hardship and tough times best will succeed.

Boxing is synonymous with pain and suffering. From the moment I met Amir Khan, then an Olympic silver medalist, he stood out. This was back when I was working with Bolton Wanderers. Phil Richards was the head of fitness at Bolton and brought me in to assist him. In addition to coaching teams like Leicester, he was also Amir's trainer. Phil would bring me with him when he went on the road during his days off, and I would sit in on his consultations with some of the great Leicester Tiger players of the era. Amir had an incredible pain threshold. But what was most unique was how he never allowed his facial expression to change, no matter how hard Phil pushed him.

"MAKE YOUR GAME FACE YOUR EVERYDAY FACE."

I distinctly remember one session that combined weighted chin-ups with heavy farmer's walks that would've crushed most athletes. Amir fought through it without complaining and with no external sign of discomfort. His work ethic was so strong that he seemed to welcome whatever challenges Phil threw at him, no matter how unpleasant they must have seemed at the time. Years later when I worked with Bernard Dunne (another boxing world champion who is normally full of energy and has a very expressive face), I saw the same stony mask come over him when business began. Many wouldn't even notice this, but the potency of self-talk extends to self-projection. In conflict it's even more important because your opponent can't hear your own internal monologue, so you have to project power.

How a player is going to approach adversity can sometimes be determined by testing them away from the game, and I'm not talking about hard strength training. When a young academy player came to his team, Tony Smith, the rugby league coach, would have them serve a short apprenticeship at a builder's yard or in another manual trade. Then he'd ask the employer to grade the player at the end of this trial period. The main things Tony was interested in were timekeeping, attitude, and willingness to learn – not their practical skills. He wanted every one of his players to take pride in their work and have the self-discipline to stick with something, even when times got tough.

This taught Tony's youngsters to answer a number of important life questions: Can you do something that seems pointless to you right now, but trust the head coach that there's value in it for you to uncover? Will you take direction from people trusted by the coach? Can you take responsibility for yourself when no one is there to look after you? It also opened young players' eyes to lessons outside of sports and gave them an appreciation for other people's skillsets. Most of all, it provided these young men with a glimpse into other professions and gave them a reason to accept some of the hardships they'd face in practice. The ones who made the cut were more grateful for the privilege of playing professionally because they'd been given the opportunity to see what their life could look like if they didn't continue to make the most of their talents.

How do you ensure you're working both hard and effectively?

COROLLARY

As leaders, we need to identify the difference between pointless suffering, recklessness, and good teaching moments. The best leaders test their people, but do so carefully and ensure there is a final lesson at the end that everyone understands.

APPLICATION

Always make it clear that success never comes easy. Package it, present it, get buy-in, and help your people grasp the true message. But manage total stress carefully so it never becomes intolerable. Sometimes the real test is not in the task, but in the attitude shown toward it.

"One thing
is clear:
that having
a purpose
in life is
something
that humans
thrive on."

— STEVE PETERS

YOU CAN'T BE HALF PREGNANT

5

Part-time training gets part-time results.

All of the senior leaders on the Munster Rugby team set a high standard in every practice. One of them, Donncha O'Callaghan, attacked every training session with a relentless ferocity. But this was common to the entire squad. There was an ingrained attitude from every player: "If you want my jersey, you're going to have to come and take it from me."

Each player on the team had not just intensity, but also an uncanny intelligence that I'd only previously come across at Canterbury Crusaders in New Zealand. They had a specific performance mindset that they'd refined over the years to help achieve great things.

Over tea one afternoon, Donncha told me that Axel Foley, who he'd played with and was now the head coach, had just dropped him from the starting lineup. After some of the younger players heard the news, one came to tell him that they were surprised, that Axel was making a mistake, and that he should be playing. Donncha turned and growled back, "Get away from me." Rather than indulge in self-pity, he said, "Axel is the coach. He's the boss. I'll go work even harder to win my place back." And soon enough he did. Donncha was committed to his craft and fought for his starting spot.

Both Donncha and Paul O'Connell (and, in fact, many Munster players) would be the first to tell you that they weren't naturally built to excel in rugby. Often, as in Paul's case, another activity like swimming was their first sport. They became legends of the game because of their unrelenting work ethic and determination to make the most of whatever ability they were given. The two of them and the rest of their teammates kept each other to the highest of standards on and off the pitch. There was no opportunity at Munster to let yourself slide because it wouldn't be tolerated. The squad developed great ability by surviving in the game and playing it for as long as possible.

"WE DO IT DIFFERENT HERE."

Justin Smith, Patrick Willis, NaVorro Bowman, and Anquan Boldin at the 49ers had a similar way of thinking. They will all tell you they weren't born great, but rather achieved greatness through unending hard work. This is where availability, not missing games, not getting injured, and perhaps, some stubbornness is key. Racking up a lot of games over long careers gave them the tactical and technical know-how to keep competing at a high level against peers who were 10 years younger. Experience is priceless. But earning it takes absolute commitment. Watching Patrick Willis rehabbing his foot and regaining his toe flexibility by picking up marbles for hours after training each day made me realize that greatness is never accidental.

Observing Frank Gore running early-morning sprints in a heavy gray tracksuit drenched in sweat with no one watching confirmed this notion. These are things you don't see on ESPN.

Another big part of commitment is accountability. The best lesson I ever learned about this was from Charles van Commenee. I met him when he was technical director for British Athletics. Charles was very pragmatic and straightforward in his approach. He'd committed to delivering a certain number of medals at the 2012 London Olympics. Even though his team had shone on days like "Super Saturday," when Jessica Ennis-Hill won the heptathlon, Greg Rutherford leaped to long jump gold, and Mo Farah claimed the 10,000-meter title as part of his historic 5K/10K double, Charles thought he'd failed to meet expectations because the team fell two medals short of his stated goal. So he kept his word and resigned. Charles was a big believer that the coach needed to be accountable for excellence in order to demand it from their athletes and proved that with his resignation. If you say you're going to do something, then you have to do it.

At Munster, I was always impressed by the fierce love of the game that Ronan, Paul, Dougie Howlett, and the other players had. When I asked Paul for advice he'd always deliver blunt, uncompromising wisdom. That said, there was more ribbing and teasing than in any group I'd been around. The players were very serious about their rugby, but like the Canterbury Crusaders, balanced out their intensity with a wicked sense of humor. In other words, you're either in or out and that must be protected.

Dougie had played very well for the All Blacks for a number of years and joined Munster once the 2007 World Cup in France was over. On his way to Ireland, he stopped in London and was caught jumping on a car after having a good night out on the town. Dougie arrived at his first Munster practice a few days later. As he walked through the parking lot with his usual humble and unassuming air, all he heard coming over a hand-held megaphone in an official sounding voice was, "Please step away from all cars." Players were rolling on the ground laughing and Dougie knew he was at home right away.

In any other organization, such humor might be considered too much, but at Munster, it was expected. Remember, if people are not laughing with you or talking about an issue to you, it means they are talking behind your back.

But that is not Munster. As Ronan O'Gara rightly told me, "We do it different here."

Have you led by example and done the extra work that's needed to separate you from the rest?

COROLLARY

Achievement in any team is a multifaceted task. Several projects may be in the works at any one time. You cannot ignore everything for the sake of a single task. As a leader, you must be aware of all aspects of your business, but able to focus your staff on the duties you prioritize as most critical at any point in time to advance toward the overall goal.

APPLICATION

The ability to commit to something when it's needed most is an important skill. This means clarity of direction and instruction. Give your staff the comfort of knowing that everything else is under control. Direct them to the immediate task and commit them wholly to its success, with clear milestones identified and, when appropriate, attached to deadlines.

"With confidence you believe you can overcome your weaknesses. With arrogance you don't even see your weaknesses."

— ERIC MANGINI

THE SMART TAKE
FROM THE STRONG

Be smart. Plan. Don't just rush in.

"Do you see Aisling?" John Kavanagh asked, motioning to the girl on the mat.

I nodded.

"She is a world class boxer and probably the fittest person, man or woman, in here. She would have me blowing hard after one round of boxing. But I would have her gasping for breath within minutes in the octagon. We would both make each other work harder more in our respective sports."

Conor McGregor's coach, John Kavanagh, was confirming something that I had long suspected. Fitness can be very specific, and being skillful in your sport allows you to compensate for lower fitness levels. No matter what you do, your basic knowledge of the fundamentals (see Tim Duncan as a prime example) is critical to your success.

You must become relentless about knowing everything there is to know about your area, sport, or job. For example, VO2 max is regarded as a gold standard measure of endurance. This is usually tested on a treadmill. However, many don't know that a rower measured on a treadmill will post a much lower VO2 max score than they would on an ergometer.

Knowledge remains unbeaten. This means you have to know the laws of the game, the rules of the organization, and, most of all, human nature. No amount of hard work or technology can overcome an inadequate grasp of the basics. The best programs I've been around always had a solid understanding of the simple things. The smart take from the strong.

Jim Harbaugh was a master planner. He was very hands-on in practice and the only head coach I've been around who would schedule everything concerning the team. He was so serious about preparing down to the smallest detail that he'd often plan 18 months ahead. That said, he recognized the mutability of sports and life, and so would write "subject to change" on each page of the plan. Every Sunday evening he'd sit down and write out the practice scripts for the upcoming week. In most other sports, the schedule is drawn up by the head of fitness or performance director. In US sports, it's the head coach that usually does this, and that's how it should be. This ensures a cohesive alignment at every level of the organization. At Michigan, Jim always had the NCAA rule book on his desk, looking for any potential loophole to allow maximum practice time.

"NOTHING CAN REPLACE KNOWING YOUR SPORT."

Understanding the game and physiology is important, but recognizing how human beings operate is essential. Vitor Frade had concluded early in his career that sports are, at their core, about people. Just like Paul Kimmage and other great journalists, he was truly interested in everyone he met. Sports themselves were just a manifestation of human nature. To this end, Vitor was adamant that coaches shouldn't "train" their athletes like you would a puppy, but rather create environments that equip them to independently problem solve. This was a big breakthrough for me. Our knowledge of the game is limited by our knowledge of people as humans.

Vitor said that he learned the most about soccer from watching kids play and loved to see how movement and spacing unfolded in youth games. He advised teams to play the same way in their youth academies as in the senior team. The principles and game plan should be identical, as this will create continuity throughout the club. This is how Barcelona, Ajax, and other European dynasties have created world-beating academies, as well as achieving consistent success with their starting elevens.

Brendan Rodgers summed up the importance of understanding staff and players during his first meeting with the staff at Melwood when he took over at Liverpool, saying:

"I believe everyone has a sign on their forehead that says, 'Make me feel special.'"

Are you simply working more and getting tired, or are you working smarter and getting better?

COROLLARY

No leader can get caught up in minutiae. You have to rely on staff to take care of the details. But as a leader you must know the game, be an expert in your business, and understand the fundamentals.

APPLICATION

Be an enthusiastic student of the game. Design your own pathway to build a deep level of understanding. Find the experts, mentors, and advisors who can help you. Never be afraid to learn more about your domain and human nature. Knowledge is always undefeated.

"The only thing about common sense is that it's not that common."

— CHARLIE FRANCIS

COACH IN THE GRAY

7

**Coach in principles and broad outlines,
but study details.**

One of the greatest defensive rugby league coaches, Les
Kiss, first taught me not to assess player actions in a game
in black and white, but rather to see more nuanced shades
of gray when evaluating game day performance. Les had a
very successful playing career in Australian Rugby League
and went on to replicate this in coaching with London Irish,
the Ireland national team, and Ulster. Les used to talk about
the importance of "coaching in the gray." When he analyzed
film or assessed the game after it was over (with or without
other coaches and players present), he didn't just rate an
event like a tackle as successful or unsuccessful.

Instead, Les emphasized the player's decision making
in the moment. He would always look at the technical and
tactical implications of an action or incident in the context
of the game. One player could make a textbook tackle,

but the other team went on to score a try. Another player could make a tackle that was ugly in terms of technique, but would lead to his team recovering the ball. The second tackle wouldn't look as good at first glance, yet would have a more positive impact. Knowing the difference is what Les meant when he referred to "coaching in the gray."

These paradoxes, which I wrote about extensively in *Game Changer*, were often hidden behind the stacks of data that people had begun to revert to in modern sports. The first and biggest mistake is typically not having a proper and complete model before the application of analytics. Using metrics within the framework of an incorrect model is akin to "firing a cannon from a canoe." The technique – whether it's neural networking, regression analysis, or whatever – will do exactly what it's supposed to, but if the model and/ or basic understanding of what you are trying to achieve is based on faulty premises, the data will be useless.

The second mistake is the collection of bad data. This is where you collect from either inaccurate or imprecise devices. The data is essentially wrong. Even if the model is correct, the results and conclusions will be erroneous, too. This is referred to in programming by the old adage, "garbage in, garbage out." You can't look at outputs without considering inputs.

"WINNING IS NEVER BLACK AND WHITE."

Good leaders coach in the gray by having a solid under- standing of what they're trying to achieve, a robust model, and an accurate data set. They must then put quantitative results into qualitative context that takes the environment and specific situation into account.

Imagine you're driving your car home from work, a 15-minute route you've driven many times. You'll probably never look at your GPS, speedometer, or fuel gauge. You know where traffic lights are, when to slow down for speed traps, and how to take upcoming corners. As you're familiar with the drive, you instinctively know the road conditions and directions, and can go into a kind of autopilot mode. You drive in the gray.

On a new route you've never driven before, you'll likely use more analytical feedback, firing up directions on your phone, regularly checking your speed, watching out for traffic cops, and making sure you've got enough gas in the tank. You will still rely on instinct, but will combine it with quantitative data to get to your destination safely.

In sports, life, and business, you need to combine experience, instinct, qualitative context, and quantitative data to come to solid conclusions.

Have you and your team mastered the art of coaching, not just the science?

COROLLARY

Are you using analysis properly? And do you have a good model in place? Ensure you're not either firing a canon from a canoe or using garbage data to get garbage results.

APPLICATION

Create a good model for your business and ensure that you use analysis in the proper way. Let it inform but not drive you. All decisions must be based on the combination of quantitative and qualitative data, and the context of your unique situation.

"I believe the brain is like a muscle– like any other it can be improved."

— IVAN LENDL

99% HEALTHY
IS NOT 100% INJURED

8

There is no difference between medical
and strength & conditioning.

"My sprinter had just strained her hamstring. It looked
like a grade two and we were only a little more than two
weeks out from the national championships. I called her
physiotherapist when we got back from training and said
we needed help.

She replied, 'It takes six weeks to come back from
a grade two hamstring strain.' I told her I hadn't got six
weeks. The physiotherapist replied, 'Well she's out of the
race, I'm afraid.'"

"What did you do?"

"I rehabbed her in two weeks. She won."

Henk Kraaijenhof sat across from me in his office smiling.

The Dutch have a wonderful sense of humor, pragmatism, and directness. Henk is not arrogant – if anything,

he's too humble. Few people have gathered as much applied data or experience in elite sports anywhere in the world. I first met Henk after I sent him a piece I'd written about my understanding of the phenomenon known as "central nervous system fatigue." At the turn of this century, the central nervous system (CNS) was a hot discussion topic. CNS fatigue was not defined clearly anywhere, no one seemed to know what exactly it was, and nobody had explained how it applied to sports, or team sports at least. I reached out to Henk and sent him my take on the topic.

Like most great coaches, Henk deals in practicalities and realities, not in assumptions. To him, coaching is problem solving. Having an injured athlete is an unwanted but, in some ways, exciting problem to overcome. In the case of the sprinter who'd strained her hamstring, Henk proceeded to use every therapy he could to help the injured athlete back to performance and execute at the national championships. He didn't heal her magically, but rather managed the injury through its stages.

It dawned on me what Henk was telling me about this situation, and athlete injuries in general. There is always something that can be done. 99% healthy is not 100% injured. In truth, no elite athlete is ever completely healthy. There is usually at least one small issue. The health and welfare of the player is paramount, but occasionally in sports, we are too protective to explore what the player can do at any given time. It's the same mindset in the Special Operations world: the job must be done. It's up to us to assist the athletes and operators before and after it.

However, this mentality is the absolute opposite to that of most coaches today. Walk into any professional facility and in the training room you'll see athletes littering the therapy tables, often with minor injuries that are allowed to keep them from partaking in practice. This is a sharp contrast to players like Justin Smith, Frank Gore, and Patrick Willis at the Niners, Paul O'Connell and Ronan O'Gara at Munster, and Richie McCaw at the All Blacks, who would just strap up whatever niggling injury they had and play on. Indeed, McCaw famously played a whole World Cup tournament with an excruciatingly painful foot. He refused to get an x-ray to confirm what everyone, himself included, knew was a broken bone. Justin Smith kept going through the playoffs and a Super Bowl with a completely torn triceps, which essentially prevented any movement. You do whatever is necessary to take the field with your teammates and win. Contribute all you can until you can't when it truly matters.

"THERE IS ALWAYS SOMETHING YOU CAN DO TO GET BETTER."

Bill Knowles is a knee rehab specialist now based in Philadelphia, but for years before he was based in Vail, Colorado, where he rehabilitated many skiers and snowboarders who often came to his office with catastrophic knee injuries. Over time, Bill developed a reputation for rehabbing athletes from all sports. Injured stars from the NBA, NFL, and, eventually, soccer players from Europe traveled to rehab with him.

Bill is that rare therapist who is proactive rather than reactive about rehabilitation. 99% healthy is not an athlete that is 100% injured. One of Bill's greatest strengths is his personality. He has an infectious sense of humor and an energetic demeanor that drives the rehab process forward. Combine this with his innovative approach to rehabilitation and it's easy to see why he has had an incredibly high success rate.

Ken Kinakin is a wonderful therapist I visited. The genius of his SWIS method is crossing interdisciplinary bridges and bringing trainers and therapeutic professionals together to meet clients' needs from a broader, more inclusive perspective. The takeaway is that we can't allow ourselves to exist in our own little silos, but must share ideas across different disciplines and unite to serve our players better.

Lachlan Penfold, who has coached in the AFL (Australian Football League), rugby, and in the NBA with the Golden State Warriors follows a similar approach. His holistic and innovative modus operandi is truly all-encompassing. Lachlan was a pioneer in using hypoxic training, touchscreen monitoring, and trampolines in rehab. He learned under Kelvin Giles, and like Mick McDermott, Bill Knowles, and many others, Lachlan refuses to accept that an injury is just a license to rest. They view it as an opportunity to develop another area of the player's ability.

If you're still breathing, you should still be practicing. It can be limited and carefully managed, but there is no excuse to have complete rest.

How do you and your team deal with setbacks? Do you stop or keep on going?

COROLLARY

We can't ignore setbacks or losses. You have to address them properly. Ignoring the elephant in the room is foolish and naïve. Always be aware of results and their consequences, but treat defeats and challenges proportionally and in context.

APPLICATION

Losses and setbacks shouldn't cause panic, as they're to be expected in all walks of life. But never let them become bigger than they are. If something happens, address it, assign people to fix it, but don't be misdirected from the overall goal.

"Coaching is experimentation – Edison did 10,000 experiments before he came upon the lightbulb."

— DAN PFAFF

YOU ONLY COMPETE AGAINST YOURSELF

9

Self-competition is critical.
Don't worry about your opponent.

Evening fell at Euxton Lane near Chorley, Bolton in the North of England. All the players and most of the staff had left the Bolton Wanderers training ground. But one coach stood alone, poring over his immaculately kept notebooks. With painstaking detail, he drew out the training drills he had coached earlier that day. He scribbled small observations about the success of this drill and that game, changes he'd made, and how the players had responded.

Ricky Sbragia was one of the coaches responsible for the development of possibly the most successful groups of Premier League youth players ever: Manchester United's famed "Class of '92." This group included David Beckham, Ryan Giggs, Gary and Phil Neville, Paul Scholes, Wes Brown, Nicky Butt, Keith Gillespie, and Robbie Savage, who all came through the Manchester United training system. At Bolton Wanderers, he continued the same meticulous habits he honed while teaching the Class of '92.

Ricky taught me the importance of never letting your standards drop. After Sam Allardyce left Bolton, he was reassigned to managing the reserves. Unlike many ego-driven coaches who would've bristled at this role change, Ricky maintained the same standards and practices with the reserves as he had at every first team practice during Sam's time and with the future Manchester United Academy stars. Every night after practice, he stayed later than everyone else, assessing what had gone well, what he could change, and how the players could improve the next day. Ricky demonstrated the importance of always being a consummate professional. No matter what your role or level is, you can have a positive impact on those around you.

Success leaves clues. You just have to notice them. I always looked to copy the habits of those who had a history of winning. The best are constantly looking to improve. Occasionally, in adopting habits of the successful people in your area, you miss the real purpose of the habit. It took me years to realize what I really learned from Ricky. He wasn't keeping a routine for its own sake, but was also seizing every opportunity to progress as a coach and learn more. What some may have seen as a demotion, he viewed as an opportunity. What some would've reacted to with bitterness, he responded to with renewed enthusiasm. The environment, players, and duties had changed, but he regarded this as a chance to get better. We all have setbacks. It's how we choose to frame them that determines what happens next. We can decide to either moan and groan or resolve to compete against and improve ourselves, regardless of the situation.

"NEVER EVER LET YOUR STANDARDS DROP."

The Wasps coach Dai Young told me a similar thing. I came in to see him and his strength and conditioning coaches, Trystan Bevan and Chris Tombs. Dai is a huge man, with the broadest back of anyone I've ever seen. He sat in front of me once at a conference and it was like the lights went out. Discussing the ups and downs that every team experiences during the course of a long season, he gave me a great piece of advice, "No matter what's happening or how hard things get, Fergus, never let your standards slide." This is something that has stuck with me and that I've tried to share with every team I've worked with since.

This fear of failure can be a powerful motivator if put into practice selectively. I remember vividly sitting with Richie McCaw in Christchurch, New Zealand when he told me he'd never lost to Ireland. He followed that by asserting that he didn't want to captain the first All Blacks side to lose to my home country. By the time Richie retired, New Zealand had won every one of those matches.

Bill Sweetenham used to put teams into three categories: the people who were better than you, those who were worse, and your equals. He did this to explain how to perceive the competition and frame it to win. You can use fear as a motivating factor in the run-up to games against the teams you should beat. If you don't overcome the opponents in this category, you have little chance of winning a league title or cup.

Is an unreasonable aim of perfection defeating your pursuit of constant progress?

COROLLARY

Ultimately, you will perform on a big stage against others. Careful analysis of the game and the demands of the sport or industry are necessary to improve. Opponents must be studied and critiqued. Strengths and weaknesses have to be identified – but in reference to your abilities.

APPLICATION

Constant analysis of your team, game plan, and performance will allow you to identify the limiting factors that are holding you back. Over-emphasis on the opposition can lead to distraction from your own development, limiting the potential for self-improvement.

"'Simple application, complex explanation,' Al [Vermeil] would always tell me.
If coaches need to resort to long lectures and explanations for 'why' they are doing 'what' they are doing, there is something wrong."

— CHARLIE FRANCIS

STAY HUNGRY

Lesson

10

**Always keep trying to learn from others.
Smart people learn from stupid ones.**

Anyone who has worked with a professional sports team vividly remembers their first few days on the job. It's probably not unlike walking on stage on one of those reality entertainment TV shows like The X Factor. You have literally a few minutes to make a positive impression or you're toast. It's funny how I recall each of my first days at the various clubs more vividly than the rest of my tenure because of their sheer intensity. It's not only the coaches and staff who are watching your every move, but the players, too – some of them who are the greatest talents in the game. The reason is simple. They want to know how you can help them get better, if at all. Or if you're just another hired gun coming in with big promises, but delivering little.

I remember Frank Gore at the 49ers keeping a close eye on me for weeks before I gained his trust. When he saw that I could help him, he made clear his desire to improve in any way possible. Frank wanted to get his own one-on-one treatment, his own personalized post-workout shake, and his own dietary directions. No detail of his performance plan was too small to escape his attention. He wanted to be sure I had a similar level of commitment.

When I got to the 49ers, Frank's teammate Justin Smith was already something of a legend in San Francisco and across the NFL. He wasn't respected because of his longevity alone, but also for his formidable power and brute strength. Justin was a leader in the locker room and everyone wanted to see if "Cowboy" would accept the new guy and buy into his sports science methods. As it turned out, I ended up getting on with Justin better than almost any other player. Like Frank Gore, Justin just wanted to win, and if he thought I could give him an extra step or yard, he was all in. It doesn't matter who you are, where you come from, or – in my case – how funny your accent is, winners will embrace you. Colin Kaepernick, Patrick Willis, Chris Borland, Anquan Boldin, NaVorro Bowman, Eric Reid, Ray McDonald, and Vernon Davis are all good people, yet you couldn't underestimate the fire that burned within all of them to relentlessly pursue a clear goal: winning. To help them do so, I had to earn their trust.

Such a voracity for excellence doesn't just come to the fore on game day, but is ever-present, even in something as seemingly routine as a warmup. Declan Kidney, former Irish national rugby team coach, demonstrated this in unusual, but effective fashion. He was a brilliant strategist and tactician and also totally dedicated to winning. On one memorable occasion, Declan felt that his players weren't focused enough in a warmup. To rectify the situation, he strode back and forth between them, deliberately disrupting their routine. A casual observer might have been concerned at how upset some of the players became, but this was exactly what Declan wanted – to introduce a frustration that actually increased awareness and alertness. He knew how to keep his finger on the pulse of each player from day to day and this enabled him to motivate them as needed.

"NOTHING CAN REPLACE THE HUNGER TO SUCCEED."

Sir Clive Woodward never settled either, even at the peak of his success with the England rugby team. He was incredibly pragmatic and no-nonsense, refusing to accept anything as a given and constantly challenging his own assumptions. In that way, he reminded me of Charlie Francis. Sir Clive had an amazing talent for breaking down games, identifying mistakes, and figuring out how to remedy them so the team performed better next time. He believed that every penalty kick was a gift and that you couldn't waste those points. Of course, it helped that he had Jonny Wilkinson to take care of that! Sir Clive had traveled and worked all over the world and deliberately put himself in unfamiliar situations that made him uncomfortable and forced him to learn new things. He had an unquenchable thirst for knowledge and ideas and believed he could learn from anyone.

When people list the most successful coaches in the world, Lisa Alexander is often absent. But few coaches have a win rate even close to what she has achieved at Australian Netball. At one time, her success rate was better than that of even the mighty All Blacks. I first met Lisa after I spoke at an AFL (Australian Football League) coaches' association seminar. I was talking with Bill Sweetenham and he said a netball coach wanted to meet me. I knew literally nothing about this sport. But by the time I left that conference, I'd been thoroughly impressed. For almost two hours Bill, Lisa, and I sat around a table in the lobby of the National Australia Bank headquarters sketching plans and sharing theories about movement in sports. Her desire to learn from any domain was impressive, and her winning record speaks for itself.

As a leader, are you stoking your team's desire to be the best or dampening it?

COROLLARY

Determination and desire are basic prerequisites for any kind of success. Everyone has a different way of demonstrating it. Some come in early, others work late. Some are quick studies, while others devote a long time to learning. But no one achieves lasting success without the basic desire to improve.

APPLICATION

Hungry dogs hunt best. Complacency is a killer that prevents you from seeing blind spots and giving your best each day. When external motivation is lacking, you must create internal competition to keep your team well prepared and hungry. The best people never fully rest on past successes, but are constantly looking for the next edge and challenge to motivate themselves.

"Our success has not been a continual series of victories. We have had a number of devastating setbacks; how these are handled is the making of a great team...winning does not happen in straight lines."

— SIR CLIVE WOODWARD

THE MAILMAN DELIVERS

11

Practice to deliver, don't practice to practice.

Sitting in John Kavanagh's office at Straight Blast Gym in Dublin – home to some of the most dangerous humans on earth – was an unexpectedly nerve-racking experience for me. Not because of John himself or his ferocious fighters, but due to the collection of reptiles in glass cases in his office upstairs. John, quietly spoken and unassuming, is an absolute gentleman, humble almost to the point of being shy. But observing him coach, you see the vital quality great teachers have – they focus on the most important deliverable: winning.

John Kavanagh is best known for coaching Conor McGregor, but he has a stable of fighters from all over the world who come to train under him. Watching him work with his athletes, you are struck by the focus on outcome. In the non-descript gym in Dublin, nothing is done for the sake of it. John is constantly asking the fighters for feedback – "What did you feel?", "Have you done this?", or "What did you think of that?"

John is a true student of the game. If you walked into his gym and didn't know him, you might struggle at first to figure out who the coach was because he wanted so much feedback from the people he was training. Another thing about John's teaching was that, like many of the better technical coaches I've been around, he had surprisingly little to say when his fighters were sparring or doing drills. And what he did say was clinical and involved open-ended questioning. It was a constant search for what the military refer to as "surfaces and gaps," with John encouraging his fighters to always probe and look for weaknesses to exploit. His focus was always on the result. Nothing was done for the sake of it. There were no mindless drills being performed here, nothing performed by rote learning.

He wanted his fighters to question everything he told them and encouraged them to suggest better ways of doing things. It was such a rich learning environment. John was never purely instructional – it was always a two-way exchange and the fighters were constantly trying things out for themselves. John never gave the impression that he knew it all. Just like Ashley Jones, he listened intently to the student. And as with Brendan Rodgers, every word was positive. Around great coaches you hardly ever hear the word "no." He told me that Conor, like many of his better fighters, would call him at all hours of the day and night to share ideas. That said a lot about Conor's intelligence and desire to always get better, but was also a sign of John's openness, humility, and receptiveness with his athletes. He wanted their insights, so he could improve, too.

What was most interesting though was his take on strength training. John believed it was part of the puzzle, but never the primary piece. Many great fighters never did much strength training. If they did, it was always secondary to their main aim – to be a better fighter. Coaches like John, Dan Pfaff, and Ashley Jones all emphasized that the better technician could beat a far better conditioned opponent.

"THE MAILMAN DOESN'T GET A MEDAL FOR DELIVERING LETTERS."

The key was to deliver. Practice to win. Not for practice's sake. Never get caught up in the aim, which often happens when athletes chase weight room numbers at the expense of skill. Where these better coaches were smarter was that they saw the time to prepare as limited, not infinite. This approach meant that every single available minute was dedicated to deep learning.

Ronan O'Gara once said to me, "The mailman doesn't get a medal for delivering letters." He had just produced another perfect kicking performance, which would've led many players to seek praise. But not Ronan. His point was he had only done what he was supposed to do. Training is necessary, but practicing to deliver under pressure is the closest you get to the real thing.

Many of the best teams ensure that one day a week the players are put in situations to perform. These are as game-like as possible. It gets them prepared to give their best when it matters most. Learning comes early in the week, but later on comes preparation for game day excellence so that habits are ingrained – the most important of which is delivery.

Have you clearly defined what you expect, and do you celebrate the exceptional?

COROLLARY

We always focus on delivery, but we must also outline a path to get there. Stepping stones are important, but occasionally we get too focused on them. The process can never be the goal. It's the whole series of steps the mailman takes to get the letter to the box. They cannot be skipped, but in the end, it's all about game day delivery.

APPLICATION

Focus on always delivering. Rehearse it. The goal of practice is not to be good at practice, it's to perform. Everything must be aimed at perfecting the delivery. This is why great teams always create game-like scenarios in training. Competition is the iron that sharpens iron.

"I've always been able to live with failure but I've never been able to live with not doing the best that I could."

— WAYNE BENNETT

TECHNOLOGY &
COMMUNICATION

THE NINE MOST USED WORDS

12

**"Because that's the way we have always done it,"
is an unacceptable answer.**

At the start of one rugby season, road works with temporary traffic lights appeared near where the rugby team I was consulting with practiced. It created a terrible tailback when trying to get into the facility. The following week, traffic was flowing freely. The reason soon became apparent. There were no temporary lights on the road anymore.

I drove to the practice field on time, set up, and waited for training to begin. As the team started their drills, I noticed players pointing, looking up, and being much more verbal. I glanced round and realized that the head coach was using the temporary traffic lights in the end zone, flashing different sequences to teach the players to look up. A complete coincidence, of course!

I've always believed that nothing is beyond improvement. I despise the phrase, "Because that's the way we have always done it," yet they're arguably the nine most used words in sports. We must always find ways to get better. Often the greatest opponent to this is simply laziness. British Cycling, first heralded for their innovation, are now ridiculed for using the term "marginal gains." However, many armchair critics have completely misinterpreted what this phrase means. Rather than focusing on insignificant minor aspects of performance, marginal gains was the approach and mindset they used to constantly improve in tiny ways – yet only once they had mastered the basics.

Matt Parker was the head of the marginal gains initiative for British Cycling. What was most impressive about Matt's approach was the simplicity and practicality of the solutions he came up with. I remember him telling a story about how they had to keep cyclists cool on some of the most grueling climbs in the heat of the French summer. Rather than using a complicated approach that involved newfangled technology, they found that freezing water encased in women's tights worked best. They handed the cyclists the iced tights and they'd drape them over their backs, with the melting ice cooling them. Of course, the team had far more high-tech solutions at its disposal, too, but when the simplest idea was viable they chose it. Yet even British Cycling has erred. David Brailsford once recognized at a conference that during one Tour de France the team had failed to win because they had missed out on one vital factor. "We just weren't fit enough," he admitted candidly.

"IS IT A RITUAL OR A "SHITUAL"?"

Innovation must be accompanied by knowledge and bravery. Matt Nichol is a great hockey strength and conditioning coach. At one point, he was unhappy with the ingredients and specifically the carbohydrate content of the post-training drinks his players were quaffing. Rather than just accepting what was available, he developed his own formula. This special blend was later developed to become what we now see as Biosteel, the sports drink with the unique catch phrase "Drink the Pink." Without first having the requisite knowledge and then possessing the courage to act on what he knew was right, Matt's product would never have hit the market and his athletes would still be stuck with sub-optimal recovery.

There is a balance between innovation, improvement, and stability. Rituals have a place, but as Alan Richardson, the St Kilda AFL (Australian Football League) head coach once reminded me, there are "shituals" also. These are habits that are detrimental to performance. Just doing something a certain way because, "That's the way we've always done it here," is insufficient justification if the thing in question stresses players out or is counterproductive. So "shituals" must be eliminated with the same vigorous energy as beneficial rituals are maintained and reinforced.

One example of a "shitual" I've seen time and time again is bringing the team out to warm up far too early before kickoff. Yes, the players need to prime their bodies for what's about to come, but this doesn't require two hours. They can get physically and mentally drained by a warmup that's too long or intensive. It's up to the coaches to make sure the players are doing just enough to be ready when the referee blows the whistle, and not wasting time or energy on any additional activity. The same goes for getting to the stadium. Of course, you want to leave the hotel early enough to arrive on time, but with the police escorts every pro or big college team has today there is no need to be too cautious. Players don't require four or five hours at the stadium, especially when most taping and preparation can be done in the comfort of the team hotel.

With the Welsh rugby team, it became apparent that getting the warmup right was critical. The strength and conditioning staff whittled it down to the most efficient routine I'd ever seen. It eventually took just 17 minutes on the field for the players to complete their pre-game drills and warmup and everything they needed to perform at their best. The energy saved could then be used in the final minutes of the game itself. Everything that was unnecessary or counterproductive was cut out. The coaches realized by the time game day rolled around, all the talking had been done. You shouldn't be trying to teach the players anything new before they take the field. Instead, you should just go over the basics of the game plan one last time and keep your interactions with the players to a minimum. The last thing they need is a bunch of surplus information floating around their heads as they're trying to get ready to compete. Keep it simple and brief.

Damien Comolli is another person who was not afraid to embrace change. I first met him when I consulted at Liverpool, by which time he'd already proven himself at Arsenal, Tottenham, and Saint-Étienne. Like Brendan Rodgers, Damien was fluent in several languages. He was one of the first people in soccer to apply analytics in a very discerning way that made a difference to the scoreboard. Incredibly attentive to small details, Damien was friends with Billy Beane, who'd applied the sabermetrics methods first developed by Bill James at the Oakland A's. We can learn from bad people, too. In fact, some of my best lessons come from working with insecure or incompetent people. Several times I've seen an entire staff become completely demoralized because of an athletic director or general manager's laziness and inaction. These were instructive lessons in integrity – or the lack thereof.

In stark contrast, Sam Allardyce was not only hardworking and honest, but also someone who relentlessly sought improvement. He believed in drawing on lessons from multiple disciplines. When I arrived at Bolton Wanderers, Sam had left a legacy of innovation. Bolton was the first team in the Premier League to have a full sports science program, exploit performance analysis, and explore new recovery techniques. Most people don't realize that Sam Allardyce has had possibly the biggest influence on the Premier League of any coach other than Sir Alex Ferguson. His coaches, sports scientists, and performance analysts have ended up being used at every club because of his innovative approaches. We were given free rein to experiment with heart rate variability (HRV), GPS, Prozone, and much more long before most people had even heard of it. Richard Freeman, who later went on to be a doctor at Team Sky and British Cycling, was head of the medical staff. Players had individualized nutrition, supplement programs, and pre- and post-workout shakes. We were also the first team in professional sports to use cryotherapy. Bolton had invested in a full-size cryotherapy chamber that could accommodate up to eight players at a time. It was so far ahead of its time that the gas had to be specially transported from Poland at huge expense.

At this point, there weren't a lot of scientific publications about cryotherapy written in English, so I translated research papers from Polish and Japanese. It was an exciting time to be at the forefront of something new. Experts from many teams, including AC Milan, came to see what we were doing and helped us explore different techniques such as electro-neuromuscular stimulation. I felt like a big kid turned loose in the world's greatest playground. Another team that was ahead of the game in many respects was the Jacksonville Jaguars. Shad Khan bought the team in 2012.

Determined to apply his business acumen to the NFL, Shad and his son Tony immediately started making changes. They hired Tom Myslinski as strength coach, built an early analytics department in the NFL, and made sure the players had the best of everything – from nutrition to sports science. Jacksonville immediately renovated the locker room, brought in chefs to cook on site, and did everything they could to prepare well. It was an impressive example of environmental evolution. Of course, it took time for the changes to pay off, but the owners and head coach demonstrated their commitment through this approach. Most importantly, they weren't lazy or scared to evolve.

How do you ensure there is a balance between innovation and reckless pursuit?

COROLLARY

Innovation works, but only when the big rocks are in place. A constant search for success must be tempered by common sense. Calibrate the desire for short-term winning with the imperative of long-term dominance.

APPLICATION

Innovators don't always act on something. They are perpetually searching for and aware of new developments. The best try things themselves before they decide whether to extend them to the teams they lead. They also develop a plan for implementation to make sure it sticks, as well as focusing on deliverables and outcomes.

"Be careful: the Emperor might have no clothes."

— MARK BENNETT

YOU CAN'T RIDE TWO HORSES WITH ONE ASS

13

If you chase two rabbits, you'll go hungry.

Never identify two targets that compete.

Munster Rugby had some of the most focused players I've been around in any sport. Everyone thought that Donncha O'Callaghan was the team comedian, but while he could crack a joke with the best of them, he was also determined to reach his full potential on the field as well. "Donners" had a tough start in life, losing his father at a young age. He had to grow up fast.

One afternoon right before a game at Munster's home ground, Thomond Park, I was in the physio room in front of the ice machine, keeping out of the players' way as they made their last-minute preparations. Donncha came toward me carrying a carefully folded armful of clothes and said, "Excuse me." He reached up behind me and placed them on the shelf above the ice machine.

A few days later I asked him what he'd been doing. He explained that he always gathered up everything from his locker before each game that he wouldn't need until afterwards and removed it from sight to another part of the locker room. This was a mental statement to himself that what was about to happen on the pitch was his sole focus. It was a seemingly insignificant ritual, but to Donncha it was a physical manifestation of a powerful mantra: play every game like it is your last.

This struck a chord with me. Only a year earlier, I was with a different team and during the warmup for an international game, I overheard some players trying to decide which night club they should go to that evening. We were destroyed in that game. Focus was absent. You can't have two conflicting top priorities.

Bear in mind that Donncha, like Andy Powell at Wales, was one of the funniest people you'd find in any group. He once herded a gaggle of ducks into a team meeting to break tension. But when it truly mattered, Donncha had a personal approach that allowed him to concentrate completely on winning.

"HE WHO CHASES TWO RABBITS AT ONCE GOES HUNGRY."

After this lesson, I always made a mental note to try and be aware of what was going on in players' lives. If something trivial in their personal life can be a distraction, how could you expect them to concentrate if they had a sick son or daughter at home? Once you're aware of such a problem, the question should be, "How can I help?"

Sports have also proved to be a great teacher when it comes to establishing a goal and aiming everything toward achieving it. A vital lesson I learned early in my career was the role of consistency in keeping players fixated on their main target. One year we decided to not take the team away for the weekend before the championship game. In previous years, this getaway had allowed us to come together as a group and focus on the upcoming fixture. But for some reason, we changed it up this one time.

We ended up losing the game. Badly.

Of course, there were probably other factors involved, but I came away recognizing that we should've kept our approach consistent. In the military, commanders call this the "battle rhythm." While you have to account for chaos and there can be unforeseen circumstances, you can reduce player anxiety (and perhaps more importantly, distraction) by creating and sticking to established habits and routines. This comforting familiarity frees up the players to concentrate all of their functional reserves on the game itself and on solving problems that arise during it.

Have you ensured everyone is focusing on the right objective that will lead to success?

COROLLARY

Unswerving focus can be draining. Giving no time off and not allowing teams and players to downshift can have a detrimental effect. Some people can concentrate for longer periods than others. Being focused at the wrong time can be almost as big an issue, as this just burns up valuable energy. Choose how and when you want your team to lock in on their target and create the conditions to help them maintain this.

APPLICATION

Do not confuse your staff with too many directives. Keep instructions and expectations clear for both you and them. Remove any concerns they might have about "what's next?" Assure them you have it taken care of. Look after their needs so they can focus on the one priority that's most pressing for you and your team.

"Speak as you find."

— STEPHEN JONES

OPTIMIZE, NEVER MAXIMIZE

14

Best is the enemy of better.

"Fergus, why are our players never hitting maximum speed in games?"

Rob Howley, the attack coach for the Welsh Rugby team, had just stopped me in the corridor of the Welsh training center. He didn't understand why in the previous day's game against South Africa, the GPS (global positioning system) data, which tracked all of our player movement and running speeds, showed that some of our best and fastest players never hit their maximum speed as tested earlier in the season. Against a team like South Africa, which was so physically imposing, we had hoped our speed and quickness would have created more gaps and allowed us to exploit their bigger players.

At that time, we had just been working with software companies whose technology allowed us to impose the players' movement data over the video. Like a speedometer on a car, we could watch film and simultaneously see the actual speed the player was moving at.

Rob, Warren Gatland, Craig White, Mark Bennett, and I sat down and looked through the film. We studied James Hook, who had played center against the Springboks, particularly closely. At this position he had greater space to run in and carried the ball much more than usual. What we learned that day was eye opening.

James never hit his maximum velocity, but he still reached speeds much faster than most other players. He ran quickly, but at a controlled, optimal speed, never missing a pass or tackle. James cruised effortlessly and accelerated into gaps or on supporting runs when he needed to, but was always in complete control. He also made sound tactical decisions and was rarely out of position.

When we looked at some of the other younger and less experienced players, we noticed that many of them reached closer to their maximum speeds. But the reason was telling. In many cases they hit these high points on runs that were not helpful or tactically astute. This happened when they misread how the game was unfolding and had to sprint to make up for their positional errors.

"DON'T SACRIFICE OPTIMAL FOR MAXIMAL."

In our race to achieve physical fitness, perfect sprinting technique, and peak power, we had ignored a number of seemingly obvious and basic facts. Fitter and more physically dominating players tended to rely on these qualities to achieve their best performance. Against teams who we couldn't outrun or out-muscle late in a game when fatigue leveled the playing field, the result was dependent on game intelligence. This was where we lost most often.

Being optimal across all areas is more important than being maximal.

Have you made sure perfectionism isn't stifling your goals of improvement?

COROLLARY

Everything must be elevated if you're going to get better. There has to be a constant effort to improve and knowledge of how to achieve this. No one factor is unimportant. Strengths must be maximized, but in context of the overall goal.

APPLICATION

In business and sports, rushing to meet deadlines often leads to mistakes. A global view cannot be ignored. Often the intentional or unintentional attempt to maximize one aspect is at the expense of the overarching aim. Keep everything in mind and, when in doubt, look at the actual game, not just small elements of it.

"I understand what I can do, I understand my ability as a manager and I just do my job to the best of my ability wherever I work."

— SAM ALLARDYCE

YOUR BIGGEST OPPONENT
IS KIM KARDASHIAN

15

**It doesn't matter what you know
if you can't sell it to your audience.**

I arrived to work the morning after Bill Sweetenham had completed his audit of the Welsh rugby team. Stuck to the top of my computer screen was a yellow Post-it note with the words "No emails" on it.

Bill was reinforcing a point he had made repeatedly on his visit to us. The over-reliance we had on emailing and texting was having a negative effect on face-to-face interaction within our staff and with the players. The subtext in short messages can be misinterpreted and you also don't have the benefit of verbal and non-verbal cues that are such an important element of conversation. Bill was adamant that when meeting with someone in person is an option, you take it every time. Emails that took too long to read could have been just as easily explained by going to find someone or calling them. While younger generations use technology more than any previously, the business of performance has not changed, and the fundamentals of human relationships haven't either. We must practice and continue developing our interpersonal skills.

Steve Peters has an unquestionably brilliant mind. When he published his book *The Chimp Paradox*, Steve used very simplistic metaphors to explain the functioning of emotional states and our mind. Steve was arguably the first person to share how the brain worked in a way the lay person could understand. It was a brilliant lesson for me on how to communicate complex systems I wanted to implement with teams, players, and coaches. Steve's approach had two special ingredients. First, he had tested his ideas in practice to prove that they worked and second, he had refined them over many years. I knew that to speak to players and coaches more effectively, I had to find approaches that they could understand and that this would require more up-front thought on my part.

When it comes to talking with a team, you also need to carefully consider timing. At the Welsh rugby team, Warren Gatland didn't have a lot to say to his players and let Shaun Edwards, Robin McBryde, and Rob Howley handle much of the day-to-day communications, which they were very good at. But on match day he'd speak, and everyone would pay full attention. Warren rarely spoke to the team during the week and never at the end of practice. In fact, he limited his hands-on coaching in general. Much like Tony McGahan, Biff Poggi, and Brendan Rodgers, Warren coached the coaches, observed practice and the players, and orchestrated the environment. All of these coaches constantly encouraged their players. Criticism was rare.

"ARE THEY JUST LISTENING
OR ARE THEY HEARING YOU?"

The absence of lengthy speeches during training made the squad listen all the more when Warren had something important to say. He kept his points simple and succinct, which created a clarity of message in the locker room. When he spoke on game day it was more pronounced and players were not tired of hearing his voice. Whether planned or not, the impact was much more significant than other environments in which the head coach constantly talked.

Working in all these different sports over almost 20 years, I've come to see the importance of unified communication. A pitch in one sport is a field in another, while a manager here can be called a coach there. This showed me the value of understanding and using appropriate terminology. The strength coach might have a definition of speed that's different to how a position or skill coach might think of it, while the head coach (or in baseball, soccer, and some other sports, the manager) may have a third definition. You need to create a common language that everyone involved in the team, including the players, agrees on. This way there's nothing lost in translation and the team isn't getting mixed messages.

The biggest obstacle to capturing a player's attention nowadays is social media. So rather than ignore or attempt to combat it, I decided to learn from people like Kim Kardashian and other social media magnets and copy their tactics, particularly the ability to seemingly be everywhere all at once on multiple platforms. I've since used many modern methods like video and animation, but I have repeatedly said the most important piece of "real estate" is the rear of a restroom door (yes, really). At every team I've worked with, I put plastic sheet holders above the urinal and on the back of each door, including for coaches and administration. In these, I placed educational pieces about recovery, training, sleep, and aspects of performance that were designed in a way to grab people's attention. I viewed each visitor to the restroom as a captive audience where I had a few seconds to deliver a message without distraction. I changed the content twice a week to ensure the stimulus and message were always fresh.

Trust me. It works!

When your customers and staff hear you speak, do they really understand what you are saying?

COROLLARY

Player education or consumer communication can't be too flippant. You must deliver information that makes a difference. There is always a limit to what players can digest. You can't throw too much information at your staff.

APPLICATION

Study your audience. What grabs their attention? That's your medium to connect with them. How can you mirror this? How do they learn? Learn from the most effective approaches, use them to package your message, and add your own unique touch.

"You don't want to train like Tarzan and play like Jane."

— ASHLEY JONES

START AT THE BEGINNING, BUT WORK BACKWARDS

16

Always start with and reinforce the basics.

"Watch every coach carefully in their third year," professor Vitor Frade said. "This will tell you a lot about two things – their integrity and coaching the basics." When a manager takes over a team they present, sell, or, in some cases, simply epitomize a vision. For the first year, everyone is on board. If the coach is dishonest with the staff and players, this will raise questions. By the second year, if there has not been success, doubt can creep in, but players will usually once again place their faith in the coach and want to believe in their leader. By the third year, with no change in performance and with answers now to the questions of integrity becoming evident, cracks start to appear. Players and staff begin to play for themselves and less as a team. By the fourth year, if not before, there is usually a coaching change.

The other thing to look at is player performance. Coaches like Bill Walsh and Bo Schembechler started the beginning of each season with the same talk to the whole staff and team. They restarted with the basics. Not just fundamental rules and values, but also the core elements of their game model and system of play. These coaches realized that the simple foundation of the game model is at the core of all complicated systems. They re-install their principles of play religiously at the beginning and then elaborate. Teams who fail to do this typically struggle as the season goes on, as players forget the precepts on which the tactics are built and cannot adapt in accordance with the overall game plan.

Vitor's point was simple: look at the game. Identify the error in execution, but correct and perfect it with an uncomplicated approach. Charlie Francis looked at the result and worked backwards to the basics. My initial objective for my visit with Charlie – to get deep into the minutiae of sprinting technique with a grand master – was also off target. It wasn't until I got in the room and on the track with him that I recognized where his true genius lay – in keeping the big picture top of mind. Yes, he openly shared the ins and outs of his training plans and their application. But it was the simplicity and clarity of his principles that were the biggest keys to his continued excellence. His training programs may have appeared complex to the outside observer, but his underlying precepts were extremely simple. You could read one of his plans in a book or on his website, but you'd only be able to implement it successfully with your own athletes if you understood Charlie's principles and the importance of getting the big rocks in place before you start obsessing about the placement of the pebbles.

"ALWAYS RESPECT THE THREE-YEAR RULE."

Like all great coaches, Charlie knew that every athlete, no matter what level of competition they were at, should keep going back to basics. Getting the fundamentals right and then regularly refreshing them was a central part of his system. While he wasn't against introducing some variety to keep things fresh and hold his athletes' attention as they progressed through a long season, he was against doing new things for their own sake.

Simplicity should also be cultivated in team sports. Joe Schmidt was a fantastic rugby coach at both Leinster and Ireland. Like Shaun Edwards and Warren Gatland, he was very serious about getting the essentials of rugby down and regularly reinforcing them. Joe was hands-on in practice and helped players fix technical errors he saw in games that were holding them back. We would meet for breakfast in Dublin occasionally and he explained how as a school principal he perfected not just instructing and leading groups of young men, but also teachers and coaches, too.

Shaun was someone else who focused on the basics and was a legendary rugby league player. He had been with Warren Gatland and Craig White at Wasps before joining them at the Welsh national team. I learned the basics of the blitz defense from him. But to Shaun it was far more than a system: it was a mentality. He showed that the defensive team should never be passive, but instead should take the fight to the offense and pressure them into making a mistake. Shaun's defensive blitz put the burden of rapid decision-making back on the attackers, getting inside what military strategist John Boyd called the OODA (Observe, Orient, Decide, Act) Loop and eventually forcing them to collapse. Even with seasoned internationals, Shaun reinforced the fundamentals of tackling regularly. His major focus was on technique, which he was a master at.

Early in my career, I served a kind of apprenticeship under Charles Poliquin, which involved me helping him research one of his first training manuals. It was a fantastic way for me to learn from all his years of experience. Charles had an uncanny ability to distill complex concepts into simple methods that applied in a broad variety of situations and sports. His initial work in the 90s was groundbreaking.

Jack Harbaugh was another coach who believed in covering the basics all the time. He thought the long, generic warmups and cooldowns we were doing at the University of Michigan were a waste of time, which I agreed with completely. So we shook things up and started doing position-specific warmups in each group. This involved teaching skills at a slower pace and with perfect technique, not simply as a series of general, non-specific movements. This way, players in every position were well prepared for what was to follow in practice. Positional coaches were given the authority to lead these more specific warmups, focusing on using the ball and honing fundamental techniques.

How do you know you've not lost sight of the basics, the things that got you here in the first place?

COROLLARY

While all successful teams may appear to operate in a sophisticated way, generally they have simple principles underlying their play. The complexity of a game plan is based on a clear set of precepts. You cannot build a complex system until the basics are understood across the board.

APPLICATION

The bedrock of any system of play or game model must be reinforced. It cannot be assumed that principles can be perpetuated from season to season. Reiterating the basics regularly maintains continuity and cohesion. Always begin with the game performance to identify areas of improvement and start with the fundamentals to build the system.

"The average attention span is 11 seconds for pure concentration. Consistency of message is key."

— JOE SCHMIDT

DOES IT AFFECT
THE SCOREBOARD?

Lesson

17

Maintain focus on the priority.

I have always had a habit of asking players who influenced them the most and who they thought were the best coaches. When I worked at the Welsh Rugby Union, two names kept coming up: Scott Johnson and the current All Blacks coach, Steve Hansen. With Scott, almost every player spoke about how much he cared about them as people, not just players. He also took time to widen their horizon beyond rugby. While I worked with the Welsh national team, Scott was head coach at the club side Ospreys.

At Wales, we had four regions of the country that supplied players for the national team. I soon learned that cultivating strong relationships with the feeder clubs – like the Scarlets, Ospreys, and Blues – was extremely valuable. There can be a tendency for tension to arise between clubs and national teams, particularly when a lot of players start to get injured or their performances suffer because they're overworked. One way we found to overcome any animosity was to serve. Ashley Jones gave me a great piece of advice starting out as a coach: "Never stand around doing nothing and when you don't know what to do, start by picking up cones." So when I visited the Welsh regional teams, that's what I did.

One time I told Scott that we wanted to track the players in his region with GPS monitors. The aim was to help ease the transition from the regional side to the international team while avoiding unnecessary training loads. By tracking the distances and speeds they ran with one team we could ensure there wasn't too big of a change when they rejoined the other, therefore reducing injury risk. We also wanted to improve effectiveness during each game. I had a few ideas about how exactly we were going to do this and why, but "Johnno" suggested we look at the time each player spent on the ground.

I asked why, and he told me it'd be a good yardstick for how much effort they were putting into getting up and carrying on after they were tackled. He also asked, "Have you considered tracking how long they stand still?" It was another measurement of effort level. I would never have thought of this on my own. This was an example of how effective it can be to ask three simple questions before you use any kind of fitness tracking: What do you want to know? Can you measure it? How will it improve performance?

"IS IT A SIGNAL OR JUST NOISE?"

Mark Bennett was another performance-oriented coach, and one of the few who could walk the walk on the field as well as any of the players he instructed. "Benny" holds

the distinction of scoring the first try in the modern professional era of rugby, and every player who came into his
gym treated him with the respect he deserved. As well as
playing at a high level, Mark was equally qualified academically. With Liam Kilduff, a professor at Swansea University,
he had done groundbreaking research on cortisol and
testosterone in players, and much of it went unpublished
because he was always so busy coaching. I still fondly
remember sitting across from Mark in his office arguing
with him about some new training approach or other. He
was a fierce debater and wouldn't concede the point unless
you could sufficiently back up your argument.

If you said, "The research states this," or "The latest
science suggests that," he'd reply, "Yes, but how does it
apply in the real world?" Theories weren't enough for Mark
– something had to work in practice or he wanted nothing
to do with it. This forced me to think through what I had to
say and find evidence to either support it or back down.
Ever since spending time with Mark – arguments and all
– I've believed that you should only incorporate methods
and technologies that make a positive impact on the scoreboard. Mark saw that there were many things that became
trendy in sports science that had little to no real substance.
He was determined not to be taken in by such fads, which
he saw as nothing more than The Emperor's New Clothes.
Benny taught me another important point about published
research. Its results can be proven and repeated, but
insights and suspicions from research conducted can't be
published. Yet these are no less important.

At Wales, Mark, Craig White, and I were GPS tracking every player, monitoring their levels of testosterone,
cortisol, and other hormones, and using HRV many years

before it became commonplace. None of these practices existed for their own sake, but were utilized to gain understanding into how the endocrine, nervous, and cardiovascular systems impacted game performance. We combined these quantitative measurements with qualitative feedback from the squad. Each morning, the players would come in and use a touchscreen monitor to register how they were feeling, how sore they felt, how well they'd slept, and so on. We'd combine this with the harder numbers and adjust their programming as needed. It was a very adaptive approach that gave credence to both objective and subjective athlete assessment.

I also learned a valuable lesson about how to assess game day performance from a renowned soccer mastermind. Former Manchester United coach Carlos Queiroz emphasized how important it was to get transitions right during the game. Most coaches only think about offensive and defensive play, but long before he worked alongside the likes of Sir Alex Ferguson at Manchester United, Carlos came to understand that the moments when offense transitioned to defense and vice versa that games could be won or lost. This showed me how significant context is when you're evaluating game day performance. It's not just about the numbers on the scoreboard or stat sheet. You also need to make a qualitative assessment of every event that starts with identifying which of the four game moment categories something happens in.

Have you got lost in the research, or are you truly affecting the bottom line?

COROLLARY

All organizations conduct what is known as "action-based research," even if they don't call it this. They are always trying to investigate the information and data they have available to them. Research is important, but it must be focused on outcome.

APPLICATION

Start from the scoreboard and work backwards. How will it affect the bottom line or the end goal? Collecting data shouldn't start with what you can gather, but begin with what you want to achieve. Then you look for the data that will impact that. This is the opposite of most teams' approaches and yet the most efficient and effective way.

"Munster is all I ever wanted. Playing in front of my family and friends for a team I love and that's the only way I can describe my feelings for Munster. I love it. But I think it's important that you keep the traditions, like I grew up wanting to play for Munster and Ireland and I think maybe you could be motivated by money but it's not my thing. I want to play well for us and I think it makes me a better player. I can stretch beyond myself when I play for Munster."

— DONNCHA O'CALLAGHAN

QUALITY ALWAYS
DEFEATS QUANTITY

18

**Quality of effort and action is infinitely more
important than quantity or volume of actions.**

Sam Allardyce understood the need to manage player
fatigue better than almost any coach I've worked with.
However, as anyone who knows Sam or has followed his
career closely won't be surprised to hear, he went about
this in his own unique way.

One of my most unforgettable memories of him was
when he wanted to talk to me in the locker room just after
practice at West Ham when he'd taken over as manager.
Sam explained to me that he had stumbled across the
secret of remaining fresh at the end of a long season.

One year during his tenure at Bolton Wanderers, the
team was safe from relegation with eight or nine games
left. They had avoided the dreaded "drop" to the league
below, but were unlikely to break into the top four by the

end of the season based on the schedule. The squad had done exceptionally well.

At practice, Sam told the players that if they won their match on Saturday, they wouldn't have to train again until the following Wednesday. Unless they were injured, they didn't have to turn up and could have the next three days completely off. The boys cheered.

They proceeded to win the weekend game with enthusiasm and Sam kept his word, giving them the next few days off. When they returned to practice on Wednesday, the team captain Kevin Nolan led the players in asking for the same offer for the following game. Despite his initial misgivings, Sam relented.

Once again, the team won and this time the players had energy and a newfound sharpness in their play. Sam recognized what was happening. This pattern continued and culminated in them almost making the playoffs. Sam hadn't just used a brilliant motivational tactic, but also one that had kept the players fresh for the rest of the season by giving them more much-needed R & R. Only "Big Sam" could have pulled it off.

Dan Pfaff is another great coach and mentor who is fixated on balancing high-quality effort with rest. I reached out to Dan when he was working with the US Olympic team, as he was someone whose coaching I'd admired for a long time. He invited me to come visit him, so we spent a week together in Chula Vista. It soon became clear that Dan was even better than I'd been led to believe – a true artist of sprinting. He was an incredibly technical coach who had a great feel for what his athletes were doing.

"HARD WORK ALONE IS NEVER
ENOUGH TO BUILD TRUE QUALITY."

I remember one morning when we were standing in the middle of the track talking. Without even looking at an athlete who was running a 400-meter interval, Dan shouted, "Slow down and ease through the last 200!" He had heard the runner's footfalls and could tell enough from this to know he was over-striding and pushing too hard as he fatigued. And he knew instinctively what to recommend so that this runner stopped pushing with bad form – which could've led to injury or at least a badly executed interval – and returned to moving well with solid technique.

That's not to say that there isn't a time to redline. The notion of quality over quantity also applies to doing hard work well for the least amount of time needed to obtain the desired results. The intensity Shaun Edwards brought to every Wales practice rubbed off on the players and made them put in maximum effort every day. The fact that each drill was performed with full focus and at a high quality meant that the practices could be very short compared to some other national teams. The same went for the squad's strength training. They would lift weights together in small groups for 30 to 40 minutes in the morning.

Craig White and Mark Bennett made sure that these sessions were very structured and well organized and got their intern assistants actively involved to keep things running smoothly. Then there'd be a 40-minute walk-through later in the morning, with effort not exceeding 40 percent of the maximum. In the evening, we'd have a 40 to 60-minute practice that was very physical and intense, with few and short rest periods. The total practice time was kept to the minimum needed for the players to achieve the coaches' aims. It was one of the most physically prepared teams in world rugby. Such a schedule contributed to the early versions of my VIDC model, in which Volume, Intensity, Density, and Collision/Contact are kept in balance at all times.

Munster is another rugby team where quality is paramount. An interesting thing that some people might not know about the club is that they have two training centers that are about two hours' drive apart – one in Cork and the other in Limerick. On the face of it, this might seem like a disadvantage because the whole team couldn't train together much. But I actually think it was a plus, because the players and coaching staff made the most of every second that they did get as a complete team. The groups at the two different locations were also able to specialize more. Are you making progress or distracted by busyness?

COROLLARY

More is more. More is not better. Better is better. There are times to drive hard and push through discomfort, but this must be carefully managed to avoid burnout. Nothing of value is achieved without some suffering. But the focus should always be on quality, not quantity.

APPLICATION

Emphasize quality. Never confuse a person's busyness for progress. Presenteeism or long hours can often indicate that someone is trying to mask an absence of quality work with sheer quantity. It can also be a red flag that alerts you when someone is pushing themselves too far down the road of workaholism. In which case, you have a duty to help them back off and put work back in its proper place in their life.

"It is a methodology. You have a methodology so that you don't need methods."

— VITOR FRADE

TEAMWORK
& CULTURE

FIVE BLIND MEN AND AN ELEPHANT

19

Don't isolate, focus on teamwork.
Cohesion. Unified approach.

Few soccer teams captured the imagination of people around the world like the AC Milan squads of the 80s and 90s, which featured Franco Baresi, Paolo Maldini, Marco van Basten, and many other great players. They dominated not just domestic, but also European competitions, with a team that was the envy of everyone. What was quite unique to Milan was that many of the players still had big roles late into their thirties – a longevity still unmatched today. Much of this success was credited to the Milan Lab.

It was created at the behest of the owner Silvio Berlusconi. Fernando Redondo had just been bought from European rivals Real Madrid and in one of his first training sessions at Milanello, the Milan training ground near Lake Como, Redondo collapsed with a severe injury to his right knee. As Jean-Pierre Meersseman told me later, Milan estimated they lost €30 million in transfer fees plus salary in one moment. Berlusconi was prepared to invest to prevent this from ever happening again. The result was one of the most cutting-edge "Skunk Works" in sports history.

Jean-Pierre Meersseman was the personal chiropractor for Silvio Berlusconi, the President of Italy, and owner of AC Milan. Jean-Pierre headed up the Lab with Bruno Demichelis overseeing the psychological assessments and Daniele Tognaccini in charge of team fitness. It's fair to say that together, while they didn't invent sports science, they revolutionized how we approach it in a team environment. Meersseman and Demichelis not only introduced a new approach to team monitoring and testing, but also showed me the importance of being able to present a program to team owners in a way that they can understand it. They explained the need to be able to say what you have to say with clarity and show the benefits of what you're proposing. It's the same with presenting to players.

As in many current Western cultures, there was a pharmacological influence, but Milan Lab developed a model to optimize performance without chemical interventions. Within a year, the number of total practice days lost had decreased, as had the club's use of medicines. Injuries had lowered drastically.

Both Jean-Pierre and Bruno, incredibly charismatic men, used unconventional approaches. Many other teams tried to copy their methods, but they made mistakes. They didn't understand that Milan achieved success through a holistic approach largely originating in the philosophy underpinning chiropractic principles. Teams weren't able to duplicate and apply Meersseman and Demichelis's winning methodology. It lay in the Milan Lab's ability to integrate disparate elements into a unified and cohesive approach.

"DEVELOP THE PERSON, NOT JUST THE PLAYER."

The story of five blind men and an elephant is actually an ancient Indian parable. It relays how a group of blind men who have never come across an elephant before all approach and touch a different part of it. Each man then describes what they touch based on their partial experience. One thinks the trunk is a snake, one thinks the leg is a tree trunk, and so on. Naturally, their descriptions are all completely different. When they were asked to say what they thought it was, they named various animals, relying on previous experience. Of course, the only way they could've correctly identified the elephant was if they'd all communicated and combined their frames of reference.

In many teams and organizations, departments all work on parts of the puzzle, but rarely communicate. They operate like the five blind men. At a time when data analysis was starting to become more prevalent, the Milan Lab team managed to, for the first time, gather information from the "five blind men," integrate it into one holistic system, and present it in a way that allowed coaches and staff to make informed decisions. They avoided a siloed approach.

It has been suggested the All Blacks underestimated the consequences of partitioning this preparation for the 2007 Rugby World Cup by using what became known as the Reconditioning Block. While this has been made an unfair scapegoat for the failure to win the tournament, it was a wonderful pioneering exercise into how to prepare an elite team (or not) for an international competition.

However, an over-emphasis on the physical component may have been at the expense of the tactical-technical and psychological coactives. Again, you can't separate elements of preparation or performance. The sum doesn't equal the whole.

In recent years, many people have focused their attention on the success of Spanish giants Real Madrid and Barcelona, but we should remember that most of the concepts that have led to their success – particularly in the case of Barcelona and Johan Cruyff's influence there – came from the Dutch concept of Total Football. In keeping with this fluid style in which every player can make an impact on every area of the field, coaches like Cruyff and Louis van Gaal believed that the best way to create great players was by having them play the game. In recent years, this has become more popular with sports scientists like José Tavares at Porto and Paco Seirul-lo, the fitness coach for Johan Cruyff's Barcelona. They both advocated this approach for developing fitness, as the physical coactive is ever-present.

This is undoubtedly a reaction against some of the failures of sports science to deliver on impossible claims. However, as I outlined in *Game Changer,* the very best coaches understand that you cannot isolate the Technical, Tactical, Physical, and Psychological elements of performance. Rather, you must develop these all at once and continuously, so that players keep progressing.

Some coaches can emphasize science while others depend solely on their experience. The finest leaders find the perfect midpoint. Their natural inquisitiveness is always driving them to learn more. They keep challenging assumptions and they're continually learning from science and proven principles inside and outside of sports. Vitor Frade was the first person to explain the concepts of the morphocycle to me. This can be defined as the day-to-day manipulation of loading to balance the various tactical-technical and psycho-physiological traits players are exposed to. I've met and learned from a select few coaches who masterfully developed Tactical, Technical, Physical, and Psychological elements simultaneously as part of a morphocycle approach.

Al Vermeil is the only strength coach to win championships in both the NFL and NBA. He believed that a team should lift weights all year round, rather than tapering off once the season rolled around. At both the San Francisco 49ers and Chicago Bulls, players would work with him consistently, which helped them maintain strength and power on those deep playoff runs that characterized the Michael Jordan era. Ashley Jones did the same at the All Blacks and Canterbury Crusaders, with players often hitting personal bests in the weight room during the final weeks of a championship run.

Al recognized that if you eliminated strength and conditioning completely or cut it back too far, the players could get weaker as the season goes on – exactly the opposite of what you want. Al's approach wasn't just about maintaining muscle mass, but also stimulating the nervous system adequately to keep it ticking over. He had learned from Charlie Francis's vertical integration philosophy – you keep all elements present at all times.

Are you looking at the complete picture, or have you lost sight of the overall aim?

COROLLARY

While you must treat the whole not the parts, you should also analyze the segments to improve them. But always analyze in context by combining quantitative and qualitative perspectives and considering your team's overarching Commander's Intent (see *Game Changer – The Art of Sports Science*). You can look at individual aspects of performance and improve them, but trying to do so in isolation will not work because a reductionist approach isn't effective and Technical, Tactical, Physical, and Psychological qualities are always present at all times.

APPLICATION

Encourage short but complete team meetings in which everyone has a voice. Don't compartmentalize. If you're trying to solve a complex problem, make sure you look at all aspects, but create a holistic solution.

"Culture, applied to sport, is about creating an environment where athletes know that you are not going to slap their hand when they put their hand up. And likewise you as a coach are humble enough to understand that you will make mistakes as well."

— JIM GAVIN

CULTURE COACHES
WHEN YOU'RE NOT AROUND

20

**Understand that a strong culture
is influential when you are not around.**

I sat in the lobby of the most famous soccer club in the world. It was my second visit to a Premier League team that day. As I waited, I slowly noted the differences between this and the other team I'd been with earlier. At the first facility, I sat and waited in the lobby for some time while the young executive assistant finished her private phone call. I couldn't help but notice telling details, like the dust on the lobby floor, the lack of interaction, and the absence of friendliness as staff passed through the security door.

However, at the second facility, things couldn't have been more different. I had to wait much longer for my host to arrive, but two ladies offered me water, engaged in pleasant conversation, and took my details as I sat patiently. The whole lobby and parking lot were spotless.

Polite British banter met every friendly face coming through the doors, even the mailman. These might seem like small things, but they set a tone and reflected the culture of each organization. Not everyone notices such details, but as I outlined in *Game Changer*, artifacts and behaviors are all a critical part of culture. Great coaches recognize the connection.

In both places I visited that day, the culture had set a tone and expectation for me before I even met with any member of the coaching staff. Culture coaches even when you're not around.

I had a discussion on this topic with Eddie Jones in Los Angeles immediately after he took over as head coach of England rugby. He was primarily interested in talking about culture as it related to national mindsets. Certain countries have definitive attitudes and customs that influence culture, largely based on history and tradition. Such national cultures are expressed through their sports teams. Smart coaches like Eddie recognize this and harness it, rather than try to change or ignore it.

Team cultures reveal themselves, and most of the time they don't deviate too far from the national or local ones. My advice to Eddie was to make change at the England team gradual, unlike some coaches who try to shake everything up right from the get-go or force their own attitudes on a team. A way to do the former is by emphasizing certain traits instead of trying to force things. For example, teams who have a tradition of arrogance must be encouraged to complacency, but still demonstrate confidence and express themselves. This is harnessing a culture as opposed to changing it.

"CULTURE IS AN OMNIPRESENT COACH."

Conor O'Shea was one of the brightest rugby players to play for Ireland. As a coach at London Irish, he was equally shrewd. In this second role, Conor explained to me his philosophy on managing talent. It was one similar to that of the All Blacks and Canterbury Crusaders: to win you must have some players with an "X factor." In order to win at the highest level, you can't create a roster full of clones who all think and act the same way. Instead, you need a few who think differently and independently and are willing to be unconventional on the pitch and in the locker room. One such player who Connor had was Nick Easter, who, like Danny Care, approached rugby with a totally different perspective than most of his peers.

For these players or mavericks with an X factor to make a positive impact but not unhinge the team ethos, you need a strong central culture with solid values. Then you can allow the players who are one-of-a-kind to express their individuality and creative problem solving, while keeping them within the boundaries of what is acceptable. Examples include Sir Alex Ferguson's Manchester United with Eric Cantona and Roy Keane, Phil Jackson's Chicago Bulls with Dennis Rodman, and Steve Kerr's Golden State Warriors with Draymond Green. If you have a weak nucleus, the electrons around it will disappear. But if the nucleus is strong, the electrons will orbit it and everything will remain relatively stable. As Conor explained, you can only have one or two of these players at any one time, however.

Culture defines the legacy you and your team leave behind. Each morning, when walking through the doors of Melwood training ground at Liverpool, I would pass a large white wall bearing the inscription of legendary Liverpool manager Bill Shankly's most famous quote:

"Above all, I would like to be remembered as a man who was selfless, who strove and worried so that others could share the glory, and who built up a family of people who could hold their heads up high and say, 'We're Liverpool.'"

Shouldn't we all aspire to this?

What cultural experience does someone have when they visit your facility?

COROLLARY

Culture alone doesn't win games, but a great one is the foundation for organized talent to express itself. Talent and organization, on the other hand, can't manufacture or replace culture. Behavior and the artifacts of the environment also matter. These are, in turn, derived from the values and beliefs of the people in the organization.

APPLICATION

Everyone knows the importance of culture, but few understand its reach and influence. It is not something that can be artificially created or enforced, but can only be directed. Focus on carefully establishing your values, which will form the bedrock of your culture.

"If you look at any superior athlete, you will find a strong parental influence. Parents introduce their children to a sport, and then they support them."

— IVAN LENDL

DON'T GET HIGH
ON YOUR OWN SUPPLY

Lesson

21

Manage internal and external messages by focusing on both words and body language.

"What do you think, Fergus?"

"Fergus?"

I stopped day dreaming for a moment and realized I was being asked a question. Sitting in front of me was Martin O'Neill, the former Norwich City, Leicester City, Celtic, Aston Villa, Sunderland coach, soon to be appointed Irish national soccer manager with Roy Keane. To my left was Brian Noble, the English rugby league coach who'd led Bradford Bulls, Wigan, Crusaders Rugby League, and Salford to great success in the Super League, as well as leading the Great Britain national team. To my right was Tony Smith, who'd coached Super League clubs Huddersfield Giants, Leeds Rhinos, and Warrington Wolves, as well as the England national rugby league team.

Tony had invited me to eat with his team the night before a game. Brian just happened to be meeting someone in the hotel that night. Martin was staying at the hotel, too. We ended up in a corner of the hotel bar chatting and swapping stories. They shared ideas (not an alcoholic drink in sight) while I sat there in awe listening like a child to bedtime fairytales.

Late into the night I soaked up knowledge from this group of consummate professionals, who had more than 70 combined years in coaching. What was most intriguing was that because they all came from different sports (or, in the case of Tony and Brian, different rugby codes), they focused on the challenges coaching created in their personal lives, rather than talking tactics, game details, or player attributes. The biggest takeaway for me was their humility and indifference to the media.

When the golfer Pádraig Harrington met with the Dublin Football team, the conversation was similar. Most athletes are performers exclusively. Only a few can elucidate their thoughts and explain how they achieve what they do. The reason is that many of the best don't overthink their actions. They simply rely on habit and instinct. Frank Gore was one such player. Late in his career he could see gaps and anticipate breaks better than teammates and opponents half his age, which gave him a more enduring advantage than his physical gifts. Overthinking and failing to rely on instinct can lead to over-analysis, nervousness, or, at worst, choking. Frank never choked.

"THE ONLY CONFIDENCE THAT MATTERS IS SELF-CONFIDENCE."

On the other hand, Pádraig is a student of the game in a different way. He can explain performance better than anyone I've met at the elite level. My friend Paul Kimmage is a wonderfully insightful writer and a very good friend as well. He repeatedly told me about Pádraig's dedication to understanding his craft. When I finally got to meet him, I quickly realized how right Paul had been.

Pádraig was clear about the important distinction between two types of confidence. The first is external, meaning that it's derived from trophies and other accomplishments, praise from coaches, and adulation from fans. As you can't control what other people say, you shouldn't worry what the media and anyone else outside your inner circle says or thinks about you. It's irrelevant. If a crisis hits and you know there will be people judging you harshly, don't allow them to pull you down and instead resolve to stay away from the negative news. Just keep your head down and keep going.

To do so, you have to be able to deal effectively with the scrutiny of the press. This was one of Joe Schmidt's great strengths. Some coaches tend to be standoffish and taciturn, whereas Joe was very open, congenial, and welcoming. He knew where to draw the line in what he disclosed, and because of his overall candor, most journalists didn't push him into revealing more than he wanted to. As such, he controlled the narrative while keeping most members of the media on his side.

The second type of confidence Pádraig spoke about is internal, meaning that it resides within you and determines how you feel about yourself. Confidence can also be derived from those who are close to you whose opinion you really care about.

Posture and body language feed into internal confidence, so you have to make a real effort to consider how you're carrying yourself, particularly when things aren't going well. Pádraig taught me that you act how you want to feel. As such, you can make yourself and those around you feel at ease by projecting calm and control, even when you feel like outside circumstances are getting away from you. Are you aware of the external message and is your staff interpreting it properly?

COROLLARY

You can't ignore opinion. But you shouldn't be dictated to by it. Listen to your team, no matter what their position is within the organization. But keep all feedback in context.

APPLICATION

Understand that when you speak to the media there are two audiences. The first is the reader or public, and the second is your own team, players, and staff. The internal and external messages can't appear to be contradictory. If you're going to say something different publicly, make sure your people know ahead of time and understand the reasons why. And never let hype or harsh criticism sway you.

"Do as much as necessary, not as much as possible."

— HENK KRAAIJENHOF

I AIN'T TALKING FAST.
YOU'RE JUST LISTENING SLOW

22

**Listen, observe more than you talk,
and limit your interventions.**

Dublin had won the All-Ireland Gaelic football final, the biggest sporting event on the Irish calendar bar none. Celebrations had begun. We were on the bus under the stands. I was seated in the second row beside Bernard Dunne, the retired world champion boxer who was now team lifestyle coach, waiting to leave for the hotel. The boys were singing and shouting. Good natured teasing began when someone shouted down the bus at Bernard, "Hey, Bernard, you can't say you won an All-Ireland."

Bernard stood up slowly and turned around. The bus went quiet for a second to hear his softly spoken reply.

"You're right. But there are two words none of you can say: 'World Champion.'"

Bernard was Ireland's most successful boxer. As a young man he left Ireland, turned professional, and fought for the legendary Freddie Roach in Las Vegas. Returning home to Dublin, he won both European and world boxing titles. Several years after Bernard retired, I urged newly appointed Dublin manager Jim Gavin to bring him in as a lifestyle coach. This was not a random idea. Unlike some athletes, I knew Bernard would never end up on the back page of a newspaper for the wrong reasons. He was a devoted family man with two young kids and loving wife. Bernard kept a low profile publicly and was never in any trouble. Having good role models is important for young sports stars. I knew that the lads in Dublin would benefit from being around this model of professionalism and would also learn from Bernard's personal manner.

Before Bernard started in this role, I gave him two pieces of advice.

First, I told him to never be seen standing next to the coaches, but instead to act like another member of the squad.

Second, I suggested that he shouldn't discuss football with the players. "Never give them football advice, even though you are a fan and know it well," I said. "Let the coaches do that. But if a player comes to you to talk about something like confidence or pressure, tell them about your experiences as a boxer and how you dealt with similar situations in your career." Bernard continued to listen intently. "They are experts in their sport already, and very bright young men. You don't want to confuse them. Give them clues and tips from your world and let them take the ideas and adapt them to their own situation."

Bernard had a huge impact on the whole team, including the coaches. There was arguably more value in having someone like him around than a trained psychologist because as an athlete himself, he could empathize with the players and they respected his experience. As Bernard wasn't seen as threatening, players opened up to him more readily. Much of this is actually down to his personality. Being extremely smart, articulate, and calm, I can easily picture Bernard as President of Ireland someday.

While I'd love to take credit for the vision, it wasn't entirely original. While I was the sports science director for the Welsh national rugby team, Warren Gatland and Craig White received a letter from a gentleman by the name of Andy McCann. He was a lifestyle coach in Wales and said he could help the team with some of the issues they were having on and off the field.

Craig and Warren thought that it couldn't hurt, so they had Andy come in. The first thing that struck me about him was how mild mannered he was. He was reserved to the point of shyness, which is quite rare in the alpha male sports performance world. I noticed Andy had a faint wide scar running from near his Adam's apple down his chest. I later learned that it was from the surgeries he'd had following a stroke. Showing his quiet determination, Andy had to learn to talk and write again afterwards, eventually returning to health.

"BE AWARE.
LISTEN AND WATCH BEFORE YOU SPEAK."

Sports teams often bring in motivational speakers. When Andy first addressed the team, the players were ambivalent and Andy was clearly nervous starting his talk to this group of hardened professionals. Many were unsure what this softly spoken, polite teacher would have to offer them. Using a PowerPoint deck, Andy explained his background, career as a teacher, and recovery from a stroke after a car accident. He mentioned his hobby, Jiu-Jitsu. Bear in mind this was long before people had really heard of UFC or MMA. However, rugby players, as you can imagine, are used to people talking about their interests and particularly combat sports to demonstrate their masculinity and gain respect. Although it soon became apparent to all in the room, this wasn't Andy's intention.

By this point, some players were losing interest. But with one click of his presentation, the whole atmosphere changed. Players noticed the photo in the background of the latest slide and every single person shot upright. On the screen dressed in white Jiu-Jitsu gear was a younger, bigger, and more rugged version of this gentle man in front of us. But that wasn't what caught the players' attention. Standing alongside Andy were the Gracie brothers of the famed Jiu-Jitsu dynasty. Now they were listening. Andy McCann was legit.

In the locker room and at Wales team practices, Andy was like a sponge. Many of the experts you bring in to work with the players like to talk a lot and lead every discussion. Andy was just the opposite. Only when he'd listened patiently to every last word would he offer his perspective on whatever the guy was going through. Just watching him was a great lesson in the importance of active listening. He was also a master at holding eye contact. Andy was among the best communicators I've ever met, even though he could go hours without saying a word.

Henk Kraaijenhof reinforced the notion that being a great teacher doesn't just depend on what you say, but how

you listen. He'd collected so many experiences and information that he could draw on and apply in just about any
situation. Henk carefully observed athletes to see what
their preferred learning style was and then adapted how
he instructed and guided them accordingly. One example
was the different way he interacted with two titans of Dutch
soccer, Edgar Davids and Clarence Seedorf. One was out-
going and charismatic and the other far more analytical
and detail-oriented. So when coaching them, Henk took
this into account. He gave Edgar lots of details and broader
guidelines to Clarence.

The ability to listen and only speak when absolutely
necessary is one of the traits that makes Dan Pfaff a great
track and field coach. Sheer love of the coaching craft was
evident in how Dan conversed with his athletes on the side
of the track. The cues he gave were compelling in their
brevity. He said as little as was necessary to make a cor-
rection or suggestion to an athlete and kept these inter-
ruptions to a minimum. His focus was on creating a rich
experience that required his sprinters to do most of their
own guided problem solving. Watching Dan coach was a
masterclass in effective communication. Beside him, he
had Stu McMillan, a Brit masquerading as a Canadian with
a sharp tongue and limitless energy. It's a perfect tag team
of two coaches who thrived off each other's energy and
experiences.

Dan told me after practice once that if he saw three
movement faults in a runner he wouldn't try to address
them all separately, as this would give the athlete too many
things to think about. Instead, he'd concentrate on the biggest issue and once it was fixed, the other two problems
would usually be remedied as well.

Some of the most exceptional Special Forces operators, athletes, and entrepreneurs I've known are the humblest. This can often reveal itself in who's talking and who's listening. The brashest, loudest people in the room might get all the attention, but it's often the quietest of the bunch who are the most competent and have the greatest strength of character. They often observe, listen well, and have the best interpersonal skills. Finding such people is difficult, which is why the acceptance rates of elite units hover around three to five percent. Conor McGregor's coach John Kavanagh was another example of someone who said very little to his athletes and when he did he usually asked questions that enabled him to listen even more. Like Ashley Jones, Dan, and Stu, John created a constant feedback loop.

The ability to read people and relate to them is an undervalued coaching ability. I started to grasp this element of the craft when studying neuro-linguistic programming in the UK early in my career. The course's instructor explained that humor can be used to create common ground no matter what group you're in and where you are in the world. Active listening is crucial – don't just think about what you're going to say next, but really pay attention to what the other person is saying and their non-verbal communication. Try to show empathy for the situation that an athlete is describing to you, even if you haven't experienced something similar. You've also got to be authentic, genuine, and sincere in both your speech and actions. This goes a long way to establishing trust, which is a cornerstone of a healthy locker room and a sustainable culture.

When they speak, are you listening or are you too busy talking?

COROLLARY

Leaders must speak. But choose your timing carefully. When you have something to say, command the room. Be direct and forceful. You can't hide behind plants and expect to lead. You need to demonstrate authority and project absolute confidence.

APPLICATION

Listening is a skill. Like all skills, it must be practiced to be perfected. As a leader, ensure everyone has an opportunity to speak. Listen actively and intently at all times.

"You don't replace great players like Pele, Maradona, Eusebio, or Roy Keane. You just create new players in new teams. That is why the game moves forward."

— CARLOS QUEIROZ

MCRAVEN'S LAW OF RELATIVITY

23

Small beats big. Using a weakness as a strength.

Everyone has a weakness. Sometimes it's harder to find than others. In some cases, a strength of a team is actually its weakness. At times with teams like University of Michigan football or the San Francisco 49ers where we had great defenses with Patrick Willis, NaVorro Bowman, Chris Culliver, Justin Smith, Rashan Gary, Jabrill Peppers, Devin Bush Jr., or Jourdan Lewis and defensive coordinators such as Vic Fangio or Don Brown, our offense had little time to regroup before they were back out on the field. With the Welsh rugby team, our superior physical abilities were used against us by forcing us to make tactical or technical errors or allowing us to punch ourselves out, a rugby version of the "rope-a-dope" Muhammad Ali used to defeat George Foreman. These teams would beat us by managing or offsetting our strengths and in moments of weakness, exploiting us to score. Then they'd go back to their game plan until it was time to expose our fatal flaw again.

This was what I grew to recognize as relative superiority. I borrowed the concept from a book I had read long before I worked in sports by Admiral William H. McRaven. In his 1996 book *Spec Ops: Case Studies in Special Operations Warfare: Theory and Practice*, he studied a series of short conflicts and identified how smaller or weaker forces can use timing to exploit bigger armies and defeat them. McRaven coined these moments or periods relative superiority. This doesn't just apply to military conflict, but also sports and competitive business situations, too, in which you can momentarily concentrate all your power at a certain point and use this focused attack to score against a bigger opponent.

"YOUR OPPONENT'S GREATEST STRENGTH IS THEIR GREATEST WEAKNESS."

In most of my career I've been lucky to work for larger teams and organizations, so I was often on the receiving end of this phenomenon. Nonetheless, in my first full-time professional role, I was with a minnow of the English Premier League, Bolton Wanderers. The manager Sam Allardyce was a master at utilizing relative superiority to his advantage.

Bolton had some great players, including Nicolas Anelka, Ian Walker, and Kevin Davies. But the biggest force at the club was unquestionably the manager. The nickname Big Sam was well-deserved, as he had a rare force of personality and dominated every room he walked into. His charisma set him apart from all the other managers I've worked with over the years. Sam was one of the first in the Premier League to embrace the potential of sports science. He was always determined to do the best with what was available. He's still beloved in certain parts of Ireland for going door to door to raise money for Limerick when he was their player-manager in the early 90s.

It wasn't just Sam's persona that was dominant, but also his search to level the playing field against giants like Arsenal or Liverpool. Even when I met up with Sam again years later just after he'd taken over at West Ham, he was still relishing in the role of underdog.

Sam had a very simple philosophy. He believed that if Manchester United arrived to play Bolton and turned in an 8/10 performance, but we hit 10/10, we could beat them, even with the great disparity in talent.

In conflict there is a saying, "My enemy's enemy is my friend." In situations where your opponent is the heavy favorite, their complacency is your best friend. We live in an era in which pro and Division I college athletics programs spend hundreds of millions of dollars each year, but such big spending can breed laziness, entitlement, and self-satisfaction. Sometimes you learn the best lessons through losses or struggling with limited resources. The challenges with big and small teams are very different, but you can benefit from both if you're open to learning and recognize the opportunity.

What approach do you take when you're faced with a larger competitor?

COROLLARY

Your strength is your strength. This is how you win games, but always be aware that your opponent might try to use it against you. You must limit the possibility of this happening, maximize your ability, and never allow your biggest strength to become your greatest weakness.

APPLICATION

Recognize the reality of the situation you're in. Know your enemy, but, most of all, continuously calibrate your awareness of yourself and your capabilities. Maintain confidence, but never let it border on arrogance and temper it with humility. Don't allow humility become a sense of inferiority, but also don't cultivate submission. Balance the mood and awareness of the team as a whole.

"If you're happy, ultimately that's all that matters. The money's irrelevant. You can have 'X' amount of pounds in your bank every month but if you're not happy and you're not finding peace in what you're doing, it doesn't really matter."

— BRENDAN RODGERS

NEVER MAKE A REASON
AN EXCUSE

24

Identify the difference between cause and excuses.

Kelvin Giles was the first strength coach Wayne Bennett hired during his wildly successful tenure at Brisbane Broncos. Even though British-born, Kelvin was a true pioneer of athletics, strength and conditioning, and sports science in Australia, and has had a great influence on many of his peers across the globe. After Australia underperformed at the 1972 Olympics, the government decided to invest in sports performance and science, which culminated in the creation of the Australian Institute of Sport and Queensland Academy of Sport. Dominant programs in swimming and other Olympic disciplines came from these centers of excellence. None of it would've been possible without the next-level thinking of people like Kelvin. He then brought this expertise to UK Athletics, overseeing a golden age as national and Olympic track and field coach.

Like Charlie Francis and Dan Pfaff, Kelvin had forged a long and storied career by the time I met him. He was very down to earth and willing to share his incredible wealth of knowledge. He was among the first coaches to communicate that every type of movement is a skill, not just a physical action. Whether it's throwing, passing, jumping, or whatever, every expression of skill involves Technical, Tactical, Physical, and Psychological coactives, which are present at every moment of a game. As such, we need to develop these characteristics simultaneously.

Good coaching is essentially problem solving. I've frequently referred to it as being similar to CSI. There's only one challenge more difficult than finding the solution, and that's identifying the right problem first. Often, we don't identify reasons properly and only make excuses.

Kelvin doesn't confuse excuses with reasons. In cutting through the BS, sometimes he had all the subtlety of a sledge hammer. Just like Biff Poggi at St. Frances Academy, lack of money or being in a disadvantaged environment won't stop winners from reaching their goals. Kelvin changed my thinking on so many levels, and one was how important it was to do your best with the situation as it really is, not as you might want it to be. When resources were limited, I now saw the chance to work on my coaching and interpersonal skills. Where technology was available, I identified an opportunity to develop new skillsets. If I moved into a new sport I'd not worked in before, rather than focus on what I didn't know, I now noticed commonalities and learned from the differences.

"ARE YOU SIMPLY MAKING AN EXCUSE, OR IS IT A REASON?"

At AC Milan, Jean-Pierre Meersseman and Bruno Demichelis used a catastrophic injury to build a dominant, injury-proof football team. The Welsh Rugby Union used its small geographic area and smaller population to its advantage by building closer relationships with its feeder regional sides. Eddie Jones used the natural English confidence to bring belief back to the England rugby team. At Leinster, Joe Schmidt made the most of the talent available to him and tempered any overconfidence by focusing his players on ways they could improve. Good coaches are aware of their limitations, but view them as opportunities.

Never make an excuse a reason.

Ask the tough question – Is it a reason, or are you just making an excuse?

COROLLARY

There are things that will be out of your control, unforeseen circumstances that you cannot predict or influence. It's important to recognize the difference between failure to control and failure to anticipate.

APPLICATION

Never use an excuse as a reason not to achieve something. Turn perceived weaknesses and disadvantages into an opportunity to learn and grow. Your smaller size gives you greater agility. A limited staffing budget can create a close-knit group. And learn from the mistakes of those who have more resources. Then mercilessly exploit them.

"Smart work dosed appropriately usually wins. 'Outwork your opponent and you will win' can often be a recipe for disaster."

— DAN PFAFF

THE "NO RULE" RULE

25

The only rule is, "Don't do anything to embarrass the team or prevent winning."

When it comes to interacting with players on the front line, personality is key. You can be the smartest person in the room, but if you can't communicate and cultivate a relationship, then you will never have an impact. People often ask me what the most important thing is when starting with a new team. My answer is always one word: honesty.

In modern sports, players know they are a company asset. They understand that teams have an investment in them. College kids are promised the world to commit, while professionals are given fat bonuses and contracts. And yet, a college student who has a rough semester can just as easily lose that scholarship while a pro could find themselves being cut even if they've loyally served their team for many years. Unfortunately in high level sports, integrity and honesty only go so far. The fastest way to gain trust is to just be candid. Do what you say, say what you do.

You can cultivate better discipline by beginning with a bedrock of absolute honesty. Start with trust and give everyone the benefit of the doubt. Of course, there will be times when you have to enforce rules, but don't create unnecessary issues. I've seen people trying to implement a long list of very strict rules, particularly with young coaches who are unsure of themselves. Yet despite their best intentions, this approach often creates more issues than it solves.

"USE RULES CAREFULLY. EVERY EVENT HAS CONTEXT."

Jedd Fisch is a true "people person." As offensive coordinator at Michigan, he was a world class recruiter with a preternatural ability to make instant connections with both players and parents. He has been an offensive coach at many teams and was the offensive coordinator at the LA Rams. Jedd told me he had only two rules for his players: "Don't be late and don't do anything that could embarrass the team." This was a welcome change from some of the organizations I've worked with, who had far too many restrictive rules and guidelines. Jedd knew that setting unreasonable expectations can cause too much anxiety and confusion among the squad and create a punitive atmosphere. Whereas playing for Jedd, the players knew they just had to show up on time and behave themselves.

This provided sufficient structure without treating them like children. It also demonstrated his trust in them and handed some ownership to the players. If you give into the temptation to create a lengthy list of regulations, you are creating rules to break. Also Jedd's insistence that players shouldn't do anything that could embarrass the team covers a wide range of things that can be applied with leniency when appropriate, because there will be times when circumstances dictate a more moderate perspective. This is typically better than associating a rigid rule with a set punishment, which doesn't give you any wiggle room to take circumstances into account.

Bill Sweetenham had great advice on drawing a clear line between when players and coaches were on and off duty. If one of his athletes wanted to go out for a beer or dinner, he was fine with it as long as they signed out of the facility and weren't wearing team apparel. You could go out and have a bit of fun as long as you changed your clothes first. That way if there was an incident, it wouldn't reflect as badly on the team. If Bill organized a group outing, he'd try to make sure it was on a boat. That way everybody would have to stay together instead of wandering off as they might at a bar or restaurant.

Does your staff have a clear and positive understanding of what is acceptable and unacceptable?

COROLLARY

Every rule that is set needs to be managed. Too many guidelines remove ownership from team members. An ill-disciplined team is unreliable and will create its own issues.

APPLICATION

Outline expectations and limit strict rules that may pose more problems than they solve. A self-disciplined team is a winning team that will self-manage and demonstrate leadership on and off the field. They need to know when to focus and when to unwind.

"Management is a seven-days-a-week job. The intensity of it takes its toll on your health. Some people want to go on forever, and I obviously don't."

— KENNY DALGLISH

TAKE THE RIGHT GUY, NOT THE BEST GUY

Lesson

26

Always look for the person best suited to the task and your team.

"We never pick the best man. We pick the right man."

These words stunned me for a second. I looked back at the Special Operations commander in bewilderment. We were having tea and I was questioning him on "selection," or what we call "profiling" in team sports. My question was, "How do you pick the best guys for teams and operations?" In sports, we often have challenges when attempting to pick players, whether in drafts, recruiting, or from youth academies. I was trying to find out how the elite military units managed their selection. But, once again, I realized that I wasn't even asking the correct question.

"We already get the best guys coming here," the commander continued. "Their physical abilities are far superior to the normal human or athlete. I don't want a man who will give me ten out of ten today, two out of ten tomorrow, and six out of ten the next day. I want the man who will give me eight out of ten, eight out of ten, eight out of ten, because do you know what I'm going to get tomorrow, Fergus? Yes. Eight out of ten. We never pick the best man. We pick the right man."

This wasn't grandstanding or exaggeration. When lives are on the line, what you need is consistent effort and commitment to excellence day after day. It's better to have a reliable operator who you can count on to deliver under pressure at a reliably high level on every operation than a mercurial soldier who's capable of giving you 10 out of 10 sometimes, but is all over the map the rest of the time. This doesn't just apply to the military, but also to sports and business. You need the right person for the job, not the best one.

The commander continued to tell me how after a long ruck (march) he dropped the guy who actually won the tortuous challenge. The soldier stumbled to the truck at the end of the exercise ahead of the second placed guy. He dropped his bag, changed gear, and hopped in the cab to warm up, never stopping to assist the men who were following. Seeing he wasn't a team player, the commander sent him packing. Nothing great or lasting is ever achieved by anyone on their own.

"THE 'BEST' PERSON IS NOT ALWAYS THE RIGHT FIT FOR YOUR TEAM."

This brings us to a related topic: finding the right mix of personnel to achieve balance on a team. You can't just assemble a gaggle of selfish superstars (or those who think they're at this level), as they'll be out for themselves and will refuse to buy into pursuing a higher ideal for the good of the group.

Instead, you want to assemble a selfless squad in which each person is purpose-driven, skilled, humble, and, to the commander's point, capable of delivering consistently high performance. That's what we had at Wales. Mark Bennett was the perfect foil for Craig White, who was very holistic and emphasized nutrition and mindset.

As a result of their complementary approaches and genuine enthusiasm for what they did, they created a rich, positive environment. Mark and Craig's back and forth showed me the need for achieving balance in your staff. The three of us had very different personalities and were interested in various sports science niches. Mark was a brilliant analyst, Craig was eager to explore new and different techniques, and I handled player monitoring and tracking. While we could go back and forth over things for days, it was always in a constructive and respectful way. And rather than trying to advance our own agendas, we always had each other's backs and the best interests of the team in mind.

One day as I was performing an ECG test on Martyn Williams, he said something that has stayed with me ever since. Martyn wasn't the biggest or most physical rugby player Wales ever had, but he lived up to his nickname "Nugget." He was gold, a world class number 7 who played for his country 100 times.

"If rugby teams were picked on fitness testing alone, Fergus, I'd never have played a cap for my country," Nugget said. Martyn knew that the main thing was playing the game, not posting the best fitness test numbers.

Are you hiring the right people to complement you and your team, or just the best on paper?

COROLLARY

Talent is important, but it must be managed and harnessed. Often those who are very talented get frustrated without proper challenges. Having a balanced team of people who can both support and complement each other is crucial to innovation and success. If everyone is the same, no one comes up with new ideas.

APPLICATION

The "best guy syndrome" is somewhat an extension of the talent curse. Talent alone – such as dominant physicality or a psychological ability like a photographic memory – are impressive at first glance. But the consistency, replicability, and the process by which victory is achieved matter just as much, if not more.

"The Psychological Mind is made up of three separate brains: Human, Chimp and Computer. You are the Human. Your Chimp is an emotional thinking machine. Your Computer is a storage area and automatic functioning machine. Any one of them can take complete control, but usually they work together."

— STEVE PETERS

APPEAL TO THEIR NEED

27

Always find out what motivates people.
Then appeal to and serve that need.

Knowing what's really important to a player is, arguably, the most vital factor in motivating them. Once you understand a person's unique needs and wants, you can more easily identify how you can help them. As players develop, their motivations change. Younger athletes might be driven by recognition or financial incentives. As players' careers progress, family and security often become far more important.

Professional players have fears. Despite the alpha-male or female images we see on TV every weekend, even the Russell Westbrooks and Serena Williamses of the world are human, too. Many are affected by social media comments or scared for their long-term health. In spite of their transcendent achievements, they are still human. Self-esteem, maturity, and lifestyle are all challenges for these great performers.

Player welfare has always been a top priority for me, not simply performance output. Mobility work, recovery, and supplementing can all help. But there is often a challenge in trying to emphasize the importance of these to young players.

I'll never forget the late, great Nick Broad, who began his career as a nutritionist at Chelsea, telling me how he had tried to convince a young academy soccer player to supplement with fish oil. Nick kept hammering home the benefits, but occasionally fish oil can cause unpleasant burping. He bumped into the player one day and asked him if he'd started taking the omega-3 supplement he'd been recommending for so long.

"Yes I have, Nick," the player replied.

"Great. So, no issues with reflux or burping fish oil?" Nick pressed.

"Oh, no. I wash it down with a can of Coke at night before bed and don't taste a thing," the player replied.

This story challenged me. I knew then that I had to find better ways to communicate with players and get buy-in so they'd do things willingly for their benefit (and without guzzling soda and other such things that might negate any positive effects).

"WHAT TRULY MOTIVATES PEOPLE?"

At Liverpool, I tried a different tactic. While he loved the club, Steven Gerrard's top priority was always his family. He loved his wife and kids dearly and often talked about dropping them off at school or events they were involved in. So I approached the fish oil challenge from a different perspective.

As I was speaking to Stevie about the need to take

more fish oil, glucosamine, and other things that could help extend his career, I explained how some studies had found that DHA, a component of fish oil, helped with brain development and learning in children. I suggested to him that fish oil would help his own recovery by reducing inflammation. Next, I found a fruit flavored children's fish oil that he and his kids could both take. He was all in.

The lesson is simple: find out what truly motivates people and help them achieve it. Sometimes their motivations might be misguided or misplaced, but in these cases, you have a duty to help them realize what is truly important.

When it comes to staff, you can help them feel more secure by continuing to develop their skills and empowering them to improve – just like your players. Gilbert Enoka thought that every organization should be very flat and that you had to work hardest on developing the six or seven people at the top as they will lead the rest. This seems to have worked out pretty well for the All Blacks.

Special Forces units are also very dedicated to continuing education. Their commanders realize that if you take care of the people underneath you, then they'll look after the operators. It's the same in any successful environment. If you can maintain a positive attitude and growth mindset among the staff, this will trickle down to the players and the team will improve.

To help guide such development, you have to ascertain what each staff member wants to get better at. When Bill Sweetenham did a "red team" performance audit for us at Wales, he conducted detailed interviews with every coach. Bill asked probing questions like, "What do you feel about your role on the team?" and "If your job was vacant, why would you apply for it?" This gave some valuable insights into the culture, and also allowed the staff to understand their mindset more clearly, which in turn led to better player management and development.

How well do you know your people? Do you understand the greatest worry of each staff member?

COROLLARY

Leaders can promise many things. But building real trust requires an investment and a genuine interest in caring for and helping the people you train or who work for you. This can be faked, but only for a little while. Cultivating long-term relationships and loyalty takes time.

APPLICATION

Everyone is different and each member of your staff has individual desires and worries. Helping people understand their need, refine it, and achieve it safely in return leads to unbreakable trust. This allows you to truly help your staff achieve results at work and fulfillment in life.

"What brings me joy is to get the phone calls and messages from former athletes 20 years later who have led meaningful lives."

— DAN PFAFF

WRITE YOUR OWN NARRATIVE

28

**You can spin a win or a loss either way
and use this to motivate your players and staff.**

Just about every head coach uses motivational speakers. Often, they present to the players the night before a game. I've endured listening to some terrible speakers, too – usually those who talk about themselves every time. It's a continuing trend for teams to invite famous players, older coaches, musicians, actors, and, more recently, elite operators to address the team. In coaching, you see them all and some stick out in your mind more than others. Michael Jordan was arguably the most famous, but not the most memorable.

That award is reserved for Mr. Nice.

It was the night before a rugby international in the dimly lit basement of the Vale of Glamorgan Hotel. Seated on a stage surrounded by Welsh rugby players and staff was another famous – or, should I say, infamous – Welshman, Dennis Howard Marks.

Less than a decade earlier, Howard Marks had been one of the most wanted men in the world. For twenty years, he was a prolific cannabis smuggler and was intertwined with organizations as diverse as the CIA, the IRA, MI6, and the Mafia. He was eventually caught by the DEA and though he never trafficked anything other than marijuana, he was handed a 25-year sentence. Seven years later he was released for "good behavior" in 1995. His nickname "Mr. Nice" stuck after he bought a passport from convicted murderer Donald Nice. This moniker also became the title of his tell-all book written after he was released from prison.

For almost ninety minutes, Mr. Nice shared rollicking tales from his colorful life of crime. He described the challenges he faced managing more than 36 different aliases and explained how he survived on the run in Bangkok. The most outrageous revelation was how he officially applied for a role created by the British Government to coordinate all its various drug crime agencies, referred to as the "Drug Czar." He told us he was the right man for the job because no one could match his experience, and it came with a ready-made alias.

"HOW DO YOU GET YOUR MESSAGE ACROSS?"

When I first set eyes on Mr. Nice on the makeshift stage, I was conflicted. Apart from any moral or ethical questions about his character, I couldn't understand how a convicted drug smuggler was going to help us win games. But after ten minutes of storytelling, from the ridiculous to the sublime, I saw what was happening. The players had been asked how they felt before the last game and what they believed they needed. They said they felt a little pressured, stressed, and flat, having endured a hard week of training. I'm still not sure whose idea it was to arrange for Mr. Nice to come in and talk to them. But it was a masterstroke. For an hour and a half, the whole room howled in laughter as the team relaxed and forgot about the game the next day.

I never thought I'd say this, but that weekend I learned something from someone who was one of the world's notorious criminals. It showed how distraction can be a very powerful tool.

Just like Mr. Nice, you can write your own narrative in your organization and should be in complete control of that story. You should also use communication to change the mood in a way that helps you reach your desired outcome. The coaches knew the lads needed to unwind, and they masterminded it beautifully. The team went out and beat Australia, their first win against a Southern Hemisphere team in years.

The simplest way to craft any narrative is to tell stories. It's what parents do from the time we're babies. They tell tales to get points across and they let us decipher the meaning from parables. Coaches like Scott Johnson, Bill Sweetenham, Robbie Deans, Lisa Alexander, and Eddie Jones are all fine storytellers.

Robbie once used a Stephen Covey video, which you can find online, to explain how players should manage priorities. He showed Covey asking a lady to put different shaped rocks into a large glass vase. At first, she placed the small pebbles and sand in no particular order. However, she couldn't get them all in. Covey gave the lady a second chance, this time suggesting she put the big rocks in first, starting with the largest.

As she did so, Covey explained the big rocks represented the most important things in her life, such as family, work, health, sleep, children, and so on. As she began placing the smaller rocks in the container and pouring in the sand, Covey explained these were the less significant things in life like social media, other people's opinions, etc. Sure enough, the smaller rocks and sand spilled down in between nooks and crevices, filling the whole vase perfectly. Everything actually fit once the lady prioritized. Robbie conveyed this vital message to his players without having to say a word to explain it any further.

What message are you sending to your staff and customers? Are you in control of it?

COROLLARY

Use speakers and the media to project your own message internally and externally. Carefully craft your statements to the press, as they will be heard by not just the public, but also by your staff and players.

APPLICATION

The inner narratives we create and perpetuate are just as powerful as the external noise from media or colleagues. So create and reinforce the message you want to hear. Counter negative comments and criticism with your own positive self-talk. Remember that you have no control over what others say, but you can decide what *you* believe and say, whether it's about yourself, your team, or your competition.

"I'll never take the easy way out."

— COLIN KAEPERNICK

MANAGEMENT, FACILITATION, & LEADERSHIP

KEEP THE MAIN THING
THE MAIN THING

29

You can't take your eye off the main prize
and what is really important.

I'd never felt so foolish.

Almost twenty years later I still vividly remember sitting in Charlie Francis's office upstairs in his beautiful home on the edge of Toronto. During the 80s, Charlie was a well-known name in sports. He had produced a small group of very elite sprinters in Canada, including Ben Johnson. His coaching genius got lost in the media scrum after Ben's scandal at the Seoul Olympics. By this point, Charlie had grown tired of what he saw as hypocrisy in sports and had semi-retired. He gave advice to coaches, many from other sports who came calling. Over the next few years through his writing and forum, which coincided with the explosion of widespread internet access, he actually had a greater impact than he ever had coaching directly.

I'd spent almost a week with him studying recovery, program design, and more. We were talking about the technique of sprinters he'd trained. Late into the night we watched race after race, usually with me trying to see the unperceivably small changes in a sprinter's form Charlie was describing. Occasionally I'd just nod in agreement and mutter, "Oh yeah," as I struggled to see exactly what this expert pointed out.

Finally, Charlie pulled up slow motion film of one of Ben's races. It was shot from the front and Ben was running straight toward the camera. I noticed something and with little thought said, "Charlie, see the way Ben's left knee is coming out a bit far? Did you correct that?"

He never even paused the video or turned to me. He simply stared straight ahead at the computer screen and said, "Fergus, he just ran 9.88."

It was a crucial lesson for me. Never let the main thing, in this case the race time, get overshowed by something else. Never lose focus of the goal for something that appears important, such as the elusive "perfect" sprinting technique. Keep the main thing the main thing.

In sports, business, and life, it's easy to let superfluous distractions draw our attention away from what's most important. The highest performers are able to block out external noise and maintain unwavering focus on their top priorities.

"TESTING DOESN'T WIN. WINNING WINS."

If an athlete is achieving the intended outcome in a way that's sustainable and isn't doing them harm, leave things like technique alone until you can gradually and safely address them. They will usually find the best way to express their physiology, while you as the coach focus on getting the big elements of their preparation right. I'm reminded of how most people think about technique incorrectly when I hear a commentator critiquing the shooting form of a basketball player who's averaging 30 points a game or listen to someone trying to pick holes in the running technique of a world record-holding runner because his form isn't "textbook." Charlie showed that we should instead focus on outcomes and give the athlete creative license in how they perform the skill.

Another influence on my thinking was Gilbert Enoka, the mental skills coach for the New Zealand All Blacks. I knew of his brother Robert, the world-renowned physiologist – I'm not sure who is more impressive, but they can argue over that. When I last spoke to Gilbert in 2014 he'd been with the All Blacks for over 10 years.

He taught me to never lose track of the main thing. This was something I learned from All Blacks – invariably losing to them. Something people outside of the New Zealand circle often miss is that generally the support staff for the most successful teams is very small. They operate with minimum fuss and so find it easier to keep the main thing the main thing.

Working with the Dublin Gaelic football team reinforced this, too. One of head coach Jim Gavin's greatest attributes is the clarity of focus he developed as an air force pilot, which enabled him to block out all the distractions and stay focused on what's most important. During the most critical phases of games when everyone else was becoming overly emotional, Jim remained calm and collected.

Other coaches, who constantly jump up and down on the sidelines like a penguin having a fit, are usually really only playing to the fans or TV audience. While this makes for great TV and screen time, I've never seen winning coaches act that way. This holds true in almost every walk of life, but especially in conflict. To quote one Special Forces operator, "Keep your finger hot, but your head cool."

How do you get lost in the details? What causes you to lose sight of your loftiest goals?

COROLLARY

As a leader in any organization, clarity and focus are critical. In today's world there appears to be increasing distractions that can confuse organizations. However, as a leader you cannot ignore everything that is going on around you. You must be aware of outside influences, but stay focused on the task at hand.

APPLICATION

Work to preserve clarity. Over time, I have learned to identify this as a crucial practice. Know your primary goal and hone in on it. Never lose track or sight of the Commander's Intent. Prioritize.

"Much like in business, it starts with character. If you don't put the team first, you'll never make it. We drive the notion of gratitude. When the ego grows too much, it squashes other things in the environment."

— GILBERT ENOKA

NEVER BUY A DOG
AND BARK YOURSELF

30

**You must empower the players. Don't try
to play from the sidelines. Don't micromanage.**

Everyone in sports seemingly has an opinion on Sir Clive Woodward, the most successful English rugby coach. They either love him or hate him. Some consider him arrogant, others see a man who's confident in his opinions. We can all fall prey to making snap judgments about people we've never met who are in the public eye. However, I learned a great saying from Welsh rugby international Stephen Jones: "Speak as you find." And I only speak very highly of Sir Clive.

I emailed Clive and asked to meet to discuss how to develop my leadership skills and continue learning about managing high-performance groups. Without hesitation he invited me for breakfast in London one summer morning, even though he was CEO of the British Olympic Association at the time and obviously very busy. But with no benefit to him, one of the most successful coaches in English national sports history, sat and shared his invaluable wisdom with a young coach.

Clive's greatest lesson to me, apart from his generosity, was the importance of empowering my staff and letting go of my desire to micromanage. He explained how one of his strengths was in transferring ownership to coaches and senior leaders in the locker room. They were then given the chance to grow. Clive's a great example of a head coach who was secure enough to share responsibility with captains and his assistant coaches, as are others like Sean McVay, Warren Gatland, Bill Belichick, Brendan Rodgers, and Scott Johnson, who was another very self-assured coach who proved himself time and time again as an astute manager of people and personalities at the highest level.

Occasionally people look at coaches who appear aloof and consider it a bad thing. In my opinion, that can be a false assumption. Aloof coaches are often delegating better. I'm always more concerned about the coach or manager who appears too anxious, particularly on game day, and is trying to do all the minutiae they should have delegated to others. Afterall, why would you buy a dog and have to bark yourself?

"HIRE WELL AND YOU WON'T NEED TO MICROMANAGE."

Good coaches and leaders transfer responsibility in smaller things first, like putting someone in charge of leading warmups or organizing social events. You shouldn't limit such responsibilities to the oldest members of the squad, but also look for younger players who have the potential to lead when their more experienced teammates retire from the game. Warren Gatland did this with Sam Warburton long before anyone saw him as a captain. He groomed his natural leadership abilities with small tasks initially. Feed your players' desire to grow.

I learned always to avoid leadership becoming automatically associated with seniority, as this is a dangerous system to cultivate. First of all, not all senior players want to assume roles of responsibility and leadership. Some lead best by doing what they do on the field. Secondly, some players thrive in leadership roles even at young ages. Investing in player development can also help avoid the pitfall of doing too much for the players, which over time can make them soft, entitled, and complacent.

The squad is always going to be more engaged and motivated if individuals are more actively involved, rather than just being passive participants. It's always a regret of mine that we never had the younger players at Wales, San Francisco 49s, or the University of Michigan oversee minor tasks such as preparing post-workout shakes or gathering laundry after practice. This prevents cultures of self-absorption and entitlement creeping in and develops independence and ownership. These are similar practices to those that have contributed to the All Blacks' exemplary culture.

To achieve successful outcomes and the Commander's Intent, they need to be able to improvise and make independent decisions in the moment as they adjust to the chaos of the game. If they're empowered off the field they'll be more confident in improvising come game day. Some coaches who complain of entitlement are those who pander to players' every whim, exacerbating the issue.

Such tasks aren't performed for their own sake, but they have purpose. During the game – particularly in sports like soccer and rugby – the coaches can't get that involved past kickoff. Sure, they can make substitutions and give team talks at halftime, but the players are largely left to their own devices. If this is not developed off the field, good luck looking for it on the field.

What tasks do you insist on hanging on to that you could delegate to empower others?

COROLLARY

You can't empower people who haven't mastered basic skills first. Unless the fundamentals are in place, it's a wasted venture to try and get people to improve. Choose wisely who you delegate to. Make sure the team respects anyone you are going to develop, or you're only demonstrating to them that you're out of touch with their opinions.

APPLICATION

Actively empower your staff and develop their leadership and ownership. While some of your intrinsically motivated employees can self-develop into leaders, others need an opportunity and your belief. The most valuable of all the signs to look for in future leaders is integrity. People will follow appointed leaders for a period, but in times of great pressure or threat, will only fight for those they trust.

"You cannot be a professional or a champion in football and only be ready to face the beautiful moments in life. You have to be ready to rebound from these bad moments, accept the criticism, and learn from it."

— CARLOS QUEIROZ

SMALL IS BIG

31

Trim the fat, stay effective and lean.

Brendan Rodgers had an excellent motto when it came to staff size: "Small is big." Brendan believed that fewer people doing more things leads to better results. Like some of the best coaches I've been around, he always avoided the disadvantages of siloed approaches by keeping his backroom teams small. He didn't believe in people focusing on a couple of isolated tasks, but preferred to work with self-starters who could be trusted to manage a wide range of duties. After he replaced Kenny Dalglish and Roy Hodgson at Liverpool, Brendan thought that having a bloated backroom staff had diluted the focus on football, and that too much attention was being paid to technology and statistics at the expense of human interaction and actual coaching.

Though he had a tough time at Liverpool, this approach has been validated with his great success at Celtic.

There are generally three types of backrooms:

- Big, unwieldy backroom teams with poor structure. These often have insecure head coaches who can't delegate or who micromanage. Their limitations are management and morale and as a result, they usually have a high turnover of staff. Poor capability can often hide in this structure.

- Small, lean backrooms. People have fewer roles, but with broader responsibilities. There is great clarity and fast communication. Such teams can be limited by capacity and workload. The best way to develop this type of staff is through the optimized use of external consultants.

- Large, networked backroom teams. These usually feature a well-structured organization of departments. Clarity of communication is the primary ingredient for success, so cross-pollinating skillsets and ideas so there's coherence across the entire organization is key.

Bad leadership can ruin the best staff, but a great leader like Sam Allardyce can transform the most disorganized group of people in minutes.

Many coaches get the best results with a small staff. Some, however, prefer larger backroom teams. At Bolton, the two managers after Sam inherited a big backroom staff. He had managed this masterfully, but Gary Megson and Sammy Lee did not use similar approaches. I remember that on one occasion, we went to play Arsenal at their new Emirates Stadium, which had replaced the iconic Highbury. I counted up our contingent and found that we had 16 players and 14 staff members. In contrast, when Arsenal arrived to play us later in the season, Arsène Wenger only had six people with him. This was at the height of his coaching powers, when Arsenal was consistently claiming trophies and became the first team to win the Premier League without losing a single game. Nothing makes you feel more foolish than standing on the sideline with a large support staff, while being beaten by a quality team with a minimum staff.

"NEVER CONFUSE THE SIZE OF YOUR STAFF WITH THE QUALITY OF THEIR PRODUCTION."

The contrast in the size of Arsenal's group and ours showed that you don't need to have a big backroom staff. And, as shown by the results that Wenger – and others like Walsh and Belichick – achieved, it's often preferable to have a small, tightly knit team comprised of dedicated professionals who all do their job very well. That said, the level of talent available to both head coaches dictated the methods they had to use to best optimize their resources and maximize their probabilities of winning. It's all about quality, not quantity.

One other interesting thing about both Belichick and Walsh is that they worked on developing the coaches under them so they could in turn help the squad progress. As Keena Turner and others reminded me, Walsh was notorious for chewing out coaches in front of the team for mistakes the players made, but not reprimanding the athletes themselves.

A second reason for a small staff is to preserve continuity. In elite sports these days – whether it's pro, college, or national teams – there's an inflated expectation of imme-diate success. This "win now" philosophy is often costly in the long run and creates a lot of unnecessary chaos because coaches and staff are always coming and going. The best owners, teams, and head coaches/managers see the value in doing the opposite. Their goal is to create a cul-ture of sustainable excellence that sees the team perform at a high-level year after year. Part of doing so is bringing in quality people that they empower to develop over time. Such professional development is only possible if you keep good people around you, rather than creating a revolving door approach with high turnover aimed at securing quick wins in the short-term.

Sir Clive Woodward was another coach who maintained a small, tight-knit group rather than allowing his staff to become bloated and unmanageable. He'd likely realized how effective this could be at some of the excellent club sides that he coached, including the Leicester Tigers, and later brought the same mindset to the England rugby team. When I met Ivan Lendl just after he finished working with Wimbledon champion Andy Murray, he made it clear he preferred having a small circle that favored simplicity.

Gilbert Enoka told me that the All Blacks have a similar mindset. There's no sense in just appointing a team psycholo-gist alone, but rather cultivating a systemic approach through several members of the staff who have basic knowledge in this area. He said that everyone within the team is respon-sible for the psychological wellbeing of the players, and encouraged me to focus on the culture, not minor details.

If there were serious issues, you'd refer players to an internal or external psychologist. But through the coaching staff who all understood the mental side of performance, they'd always have access to psychology-driven resources. He also believed that the leadership must take a primary role in psychology. If you have a head coach who doesn't care about mental health, you're more likely to have a team with issues in this area. Gilbert viewed his role as primarily helping the players perform under pressure. He also emphasized to the All Blacks that they had the chance and the responsibility to continue the legacy of the great sides from the past.

He was a proponent of keeping your backroom staff between 15 and 18 people at most for rugby, no matter how big your budget was. Gilbert also thought that the organization should be very flat and that you had to work hardest on developing the six or seven people at the top as they will lead the rest.

Is your team small, agile, and effective or bloated, costly, and failing to deliver?

COROLLARY

Maintaining a small staff doesn't mean you have to sacrifice. You just create two layers. The core is a dedicated and versatile team that knows each other and works well together. Then you supplement this with third party consultants and advisors. This retains domain knowledge and allows you to stay nimble, while keeping experts on speed-dial so you can utilize their know-how in specific situations.

APPLICATION

Hire one, pay the salary of two, and get the work of three.

"There is no attacking football or defensive football. When you have the ball, you have to think about what will happen when you lose it. When you do not have it, you need to know what you will do when you get it back."

— VITOR FRADE

THIS IS A PEOPLE BUSINESS

32

**People skills matter more than intelligence.
Practice integrity.**

The "Boot Room" was a small room at Melwood, the Liverpool training ground, where during the 1960s to the early 1990s the coaching staff would sit, drink tea, and discuss the team, tactics, and the next game's opponent. The Boot Room was situated across from the changing rooms and as the name suggests, was where academy players cleaned the first team's boots. Bill Shankly converted it into an informal coaches' meeting room, with a relaxing atmosphere where he, Bob Paisley, Reuben Bennett, Tom Saunders, Joe Fagan, and Ronnie Moran sat around and chatted like teachers in a breakroom. Some of the greatest ideas came out of these impromptu conversations.

We sometimes forget that professional players are also fans, and Stephen Jones, the legendary Welsh fly-half, was a huge Liverpool supporter. One day I arranged for us both to go up to Melwood to watch practice. Of course, not being the brightest light bulbs in the room, dumb and dumber arrived on a wet, windy day without jackets. We stood by the door of the facility next to the famous Boot Room and watched players jogging out to warm up.

Suddenly, a voice came from behind us. "No jackets guys? Come here." We turned around to see Kenny Dalglish, Liverpool head coach, standing in the doorway. He walked back inside the building, went into the coaches' locker room, and returned with two large coats. Here was one of the greatest soccer players and coaches of all time noticing two strangers underdressed, when it would have been easier to just stroll past. Who wouldn't want to play or work for a coach like that?

As we sat upstairs after practice, Stephen and I looked down over the Melwood training fields and watched a player working with a coach after practice. He was running from the half way line, passing a ball to the coach on the edge of the box, taking the return pass, and shooting at the empty net. His return was poor, with balls going high and wide, left and right, but not in the goal. When Kenny joined us upstairs, we asked who the player was. Kenny told us it was a new Uruguayan player they had just signed. When Kenny left, Stephen and I both looked at each other and agreed this Luis Suárez guy was never going to make it. Shows you what we knew!

Kenny's example emphasizes that coaching and managing is a people business. Beyond all the hype, stats, and fancy gadgets, we ultimately thrive on our relationships with others. When I was at the 49ers, Eric Mangini knew I'd be alone over the Christmas break. He made a point of inviting me to his house to have dinner with him, offensive coordinator Greg

Roman, and their families on Christmas Eve. When I left the Niners, the first calls on my phone were from Frank Gore, Justin Smith, Vernon Davis, and Colin Kaepernick. Coaching is a subset of life. Life isn't a subset of coaching.

Sometimes such a caring attitude is born out of hardship. Your own tough experiences can fine-tune you to what others are experiencing and make you more empathetic toward them. Eddie Jones dealt with racist taunts and bullying as a kid and player. This has always given him a different perspective on the player's experience. He's certainly no-nonsense in his approach, but this can often mask his underlying sensitivity. Eddie is tough and abrupt. Yet he has a deep empathy with his players and staff that makes him very endearing. Many of the best coaches share this quality. Dan Pfaff, Ricky Sbragia, Shaun Edwards, Don Brown, Brendan Rodgers, Declan Kidney, and Biff Poggi all care deeply about each and every athlete they work with.

I've also come across a lot of players who are very people-focused and went on to be great coaches. Colin Kaepernick would always make a point of speaking to every single person – from team owner to janitor – in the same considerate way, turning to face them and giving them his full attention, a rare occurrence in any arena. Someone similar who made an impression on me at Bolton Wanderers was Gary Speed. He was a great player, having captained Wales and Bolton in the Premier League and later becoming the Welsh coach. But he was an even better human being. Players like Gary who have movie star looks and all the talent in the world can often be aloof, but he was caring, thoughtful, and considerate to a fault.

Years after we'd both left the team, I was walking through the lobby in the Vale of Glamorgan Hotel with the Welsh Rugby team and heard someone call out, "Hey, Fergus!" I spun around to see Gary standing there. He asked me how I was doing, and we spent a few minutes catching up. He invited me to meet with him again at breakfast the next morning with Raymond Verheijen and Damian Roden, who I'd coached with at Bolton. Gary never forgot anyone and was genuinely invested in everybody around him. His early passing was a big shock to me and I'll always remember him being a true gentleman.

"WINNING IS ALWAYS A PEOPLE BUSINESS."

Charisma is not in short supply in the sports world. I've learned so much from meeting people like ESPN's Adam Schefter – a bundle of charisma in his own right far away from the camera and Eddie McGuire, president of Collingwood Football Club, but no one has more charisma than Sam Allardyce. There's a reason he is called Big Sam, and it's not just his imposing physical stature. His personality is unique. After I left Bolton, I continued to work one-on-one with a few of the players. One of these was the Irish international Joey O'Brien. During the season I would stay with Joey, do manual therapy to sort his body out, give him some additional speed work, and ensure his food was prepared properly for games. As the great sprint coach Dan Pfaff often says, "We can't truly fix things, we can only manage them."

Joey had been dealing with a knee issue at Bolton for years. Of course, his professionalism was impressive, but I also admired how Sam managed Joey's load. As Joey worked to regain his fitness, Sam didn't rush him back or overwork him in training. And it wasn't just Joey. Sam also got the most out of older players like Gary Speed, Jussi

Jääskeläinen, Jay-Jay Okocha, Kevin Davies, Iván Campo, Stelios Giannakopoulos, Kevin Nolan, Nicky Hunt, Henrik Pedersen, Ricardo Gardner, and El Hadji Diouf.

One day after Joey had returned from a successful loan spell, Sam called Joey into his office and told him that Sheffield Wednesday wanted to sign him from Bolton. He asked Joey what he thought about it. Did he want to stay at Bolton or leave for a new club?

At the time, Sheffield Wednesday were in League One, the division below, and Joey might've gotten more playing time there. When Joey hesitated, Sam said, "Remember that the Premier League is the only one that counts, Joey." And sure enough, Joey stayed at Bolton.

Sam was making it clear to Joey that you have to play at the highest level against the best competition to keep improving as your career progresses. Sure, nobody wants to be stuck on the bench for any team and everyone wants playing time, but you need to balance this against the reality that athletes improve to the level they compete against. If you want to be the best, you have to be around the best.

Alan "Thumper" Phillips was the team manager while I was at Wales. This role is unique to rugby. The head coach actually oversees the team, while it's up to the team manager to ensure he can do that. It would be a very helpful role in US sports and an important one because it involves both serving and helping manage the head coach and team. Thumper played 18 times for Wales and toured with the British Lions. He has a unique sense of humor, is an excellent people person, and knows how to manage players. Every time the team stayed at a hotel, Thumper presented the manager with a signed squad photo just before we left. He knew that at some stage we'd likely return, and it was important to express gratitude to everyone who looked after the team so they'd do it again next time. This went for drivers, chefs, and anyone in a service role. Thumper understood that everyone who came in contact with the team had important and influential roles in their own way.

Those in the Special Operations community recognized this a long time ago and it helped coin the phrase "hearts and minds." Some units understand it better than others. They too appreciate that support staff are the ones you turn to first when something goes wrong, as it often does in battle and during training exercises. When I visited Milan, I spent some time with a couple of team doctors who showed me old faded yellow printouts of ECG/EKGs they had done on AC Milan's youth players as far back as the 60s. Then as now, the priority was overall health, not just on-field performance.

At times, the sports industry can be ruthless and very competitive. People can be nasty, disparaging, and self-focused. I was hit quite hard with an important lesson shortly after I had visited the Canterbury Crusaders. Luke Thornley, a young assistant strength coach, had died tragically. It naturally affected the whole organization deeply. Even though I'd only been around Luke for a few weeks, I was left asking myself what I'd missed or could have done to help him. Before you send a tweet or post a message, it's worth bearing in mind that you rarely know what others are dealing with. Ashley Jones gave me a carving of Te Manaia (the Maori guardian spirit), which I keep on my desk at home as a reminder that we are all guardians of each other in this business.

Are you taking care of your most important asset?

COROLLARY

Life, coaching, the military, and the corporate world are all people businesses.

APPLICATION

Those who choose to treat people poorly in sports or business never succeed in the long run. Short-term success at the expense of decency leads to distrust, paranoia, and high staff turnover, resulting in low loyalty, insecurity, and suspicion. Despite outward appearances, even the most ebullient people can have personal lives that are in turmoil. So always strive to be kind.

"Arrogance is only bad when you lose. If you are winning and you are arrogant, then it is self-belief."

— EDDIE JONES

THIN LINE BETWEEN DELEGATION AND ABDICATION

33

Manage, but don't impose. Stay in control.

I first heard Australian rugby coach Scott Johnson say, "There's a thin line between delegation and abdication." In my experience, some of the best coaches are those who empower their staff and players. Carlos Queiroz told me that he thought this was one of Sir Alex Ferguson's greatest assets. He knew what was going on in every aspect of the organization, but invested responsibility in others and trusted them to do what they did best. While Ferguson was a very commanding presence and didn't suffer fools, he refused to interfere with or micromanage his staff. Scott Johnson was a firm believer in trust-based delegation, too. He taught me that you must hand off some responsibilities because the head coach can never deal with everything. Yet you cannot give away responsibility. You've got to know what's going on in each area, but trust your assistant coaches to be the experts and do what they do best. As a leader, the buck stops with you. Scott had no problem taking responsibility for errors his players or coaches made and did his best to deflect scrutiny and criticism away from them by putting himself in the firing line.

Wales rugby head coach Warren Gatland saw leadership potential in Sam Warburton long before he was a regular at club level. I clearly remember the first time Warren asked Sam to critique the defensive tackling of the previous game, one he hadn't even started in. Sam delivered his analysis with uncanny clarity and precision. This was the start of the pathway for "Warby" to eventually captain Wales and later the British and Irish Lions.

Some people suggest leaders are born, not made. I couldn't disagree more. They are revealed. First, not all leaders are good people, or the right ones to lead a team or group. Many men and women have leadership qualities. Some need support and others simply require an opportunity to prove themselves. If you as a coach don't manage the leadership process carefully or allow a vacuum to develop, you'll often have the wrong type of leader fill it. In truth, the ideal scenario is that everyone becomes a leader and is encouraged to act as such.

"MANAGE WITHOUT INTERFERENCE."

I've often seen organizations in which the head coach has a larger-than-life personality, oversized ego, or just craves attention. In these cases, ownership is rarely transferred to the team. When things go wrong during a game, players are left looking at each other for direction – or worse still, turning to the sideline for an answer. The best coaches delegate and empower players. They start with small tasks to test and grow leadership qualities and then progress, like Warren did with Sam, to entrusting player-leaders with greater responsibility. This develops the player's confidence in demonstrating leadership to their teammates. Finally, good coaches watch the response of the other players to the proposed captain to see if they respond, engage, and act positively.

Coaching and sports in general can be ego-driven. Someone who is egotistical is often lacking in self-esteem and is deeply insecure, which is why they behave the way they do. It's important for a coach to feel confident in their own abilities and with themselves as a person, as this will make it easier for them to stay humble and trust the expertise of those around them. In addition, the head coach must also think about the security and desires of their staff. These people need to be continually developed and given the opportunity to progress and grow. Otherwise their careers will stagnate, and they'll start to look elsewhere for fresh opportunities. A great coach not only surrounds themselves with good people, but also goes out of their way to make them better.

One time I was speaking with Graham Henry after we lost to the All Blacks (again) and I asked him about leadership of the players on the field. He said, "Remember that I used to be a headmaster, and that showed me how little control I had over students." It was a vital lesson to me about decentralization of learning, the futility of micromanagement, and the need to foster independent decision making among players.

Is your leadership present, but not overbearing? Are you aware of everything that's going on?

COROLLARY

You might not have ready-made leaders. In which case, you'll need to lead and provide direction initially. But you will only do this temporarily to allow team members time and space to develop and find their real leaders.

APPLICATION

Always build leaders. Never allow one or two to assume leadership exclusively. Teams change and injuries happen. It is then you find out who can step up, but this must be deliberately cultivated. Be careful who you choose, as teams take on the character of those who lead them.

"Make your hard days hard and your easy days easy."

— CHARLIE FRANCIS

THERE IS NO SUCH THING AS DISCIPLINE

Lesson

34

Self-discipline and self-confidence exist, discipline and confidence cannot be given or imposed.

Strolling through a top secret military base, I debated a great dichotomy in elite performance with a highly decorated commander: how do you balance discipline and talent and structure with fluidity? The great All Black Tana Umaga had just begun his coaching career and when he called me to talk about coaching methods, I'd asked him a similar question: How do you install a disciplined game plan and yet still allow players to express themselves? Few teams can manage this well, but great ones find a way. Tana's answer was simple: include the players in any disciplinary process.

As the commander and I walked from one compound to the other in the crisp spring air, he explained to me that in the elite units, the challenge is to create leaders who can think for themselves. In most (but not all) cases, the operator they are preparing has been taught to take orders and instructions without question up until they get to his unit. However, especially as conflict has become much more unconventional, a need has arisen to develop independent operators who can think and act with ingenuity in highly unpredictable situations. He explained the balancing act of discipline and the freedom to improvise through the analogy of a piece of litter.

Firstly, there is no such thing as external discipline with elite performers, only self-discipline. If the operator doesn't do it because they choose to, then they are not thinking independently. If operators just do what they are told unquestioningly, it's merely rote learning at that point and there is no understanding of the value of the action. When the instructor isn't there, the real purpose of the lesson is not learned. Discipline is what you do at the behest of someone else, while self-discipline is when you do it on your own initiative.

Secondly, as a leader, you can't control everything. You should provide a framework for only some things and give the operator limited guidance so they can decide how best to achieve the aim in any given situation. This is why in all my consulting work I emphasize principles and heuristics, never rules.

We stopped walking for a moment as the commander bent down to pick up a piece of a torn Styrofoam cup that was lying by the edge of the path. "We have a rule that you never walk past a piece of litter," he explained. "The purpose is simple. We tell our operators that even when you're out with friends, you are different. Never walking past a piece of litter is a reminder that you are not above anyone else. You're a servant and must always remember who you are."

"DON'T FORCE OBEDIENCE THROUGH INTIMIDATION. INSPIRE SELF-DISCIPLINE INSTEAD."

It was an elegant guiding principle for life: serve and always remain vigilant. This lesson has stuck with me. I refuse to ignore trash on the ground. "Never walk past a piece of litter" is not a rule per se, but rather a way to remind you repeatedly on a daily basis that you are different and on a path of relentless self-discipline.

Someone else who emphasized self-discipline was Wayne Bennett. Simply meeting him was a study in coaching greatness. There was a grandfatherly aura about Wayne, but an unmistakable steeliness, too. Cautious and reserved with a wicked sense of humor, he had a watchful eye that misses nothing. Wayne was constantly watching everything and everybody around him. Assistant coaches and players will tell you about how he'd subtly raise things that everyone else missed or didn't notice. Everything he did had a reason.

When an assistant coach once put a fine notice on the wall to warn players against tardiness, he asked them to take it down. Wayne explained that he didn't want to put unnecessary restrictions on the players. If the coach had a problem with an individual, he would go to him and sort it out. Unless it was a serious issue, Wayne didn't need to know.

Joe Schmidt didn't impose his personality on his players or force them to align with his vision. Instead, he invested time to get to know them as people, and then saw how best to deal with each individual. Yes, he had firm principles that he believed in, but he also allowed players to be themselves. Two teams can be very evenly matched physically and it's often those who encourage individuality and innovation that take home the trophy.

How do you ensure you haven't created an atmosphere of fear, which kills happiness and inspiration?

COROLLARY

People are not born with self-discipline, so at the beginning it occasionally must be demonstrated and explained to them, and sometimes enforced. Any discipline must be carefully imposed, however. Introduce it in a way that leads to self-discipline.

APPLICATION

Encourage discipline in a way that develops people and enriches their lives. Empower them to take ownership of what they do and give the organization ownership, too, by including players or staff in the disciplinary process.

"Know that
you have
complete
control over
what you put
in your mouth.
No one ever
ate anything
by accident."

— CHARLES POLIQUIN

THE TALENT CURSE

35

You need a few men to carry the piano,
but only one to play it.

In 2008, the AFL (Australian Football League) decided to add
two clubs to its ranks. Four years later, Greater Western
Sydney (GWS) Giants, announced Kevin Sheedy as its senior
coach, with Leon Cameron and Alan McConnell as his assistants. To help the team get started in the league, GWS received
preferential recruitment entitlements (a combination of
American sports drafting and trading), as did the Gold Coast
Suns who had entered the AFL the year before. Sometime
after the team was established, I was asked by the AFL to
audit them to help highlight areas of potential improvement.

This audit was more interesting than many others I'd
done because of one major difference between how the
new teams created their rosters. While the Gold Coast
Suns traded some draft picks and went after established
stars such as Gary Ablett Jr., GWS built through the draft,

picking up very talented young players and constructing a new, but, obviously, very inexperienced roster.

On paper, getting the best draft picks would seem to make a lot of sense. Afterall, skillful players are always at a premium. Strength, endurance, and power can be worked on, but skill and natural athleticism are incredibly hard to develop, if not impossible. The case study of the Giants was fascinating. Perhaps predictably, they struggled at the beginning. The young players and coaching staff, though extremely talented, were finding it hard to compete with physically dominant teams who often intimidated them or played tactically smarter games. As this trend continued, team morale and confidence was stretched to the limit. They didn't hide from their growing pains, though. In many cases, leaders try to solve issues themselves, but teams like GWS who are committed to Carol Dweck's growth mindset include players in the process and talk through the challenges, keeping team spirit and focus alive.

Rarely is there an opportunity to study firsthand a situation where raw talent is pitted against experience. This is the talent curse. Occasionally, young teams or players with great ability have not experienced hardship. In their youth and with their superior athleticism, size, or skill in their age group, they are used to outshining opponents. Yet when these players move to professional or senior level, the demands of the game change and a completely new unexpected challenge is presented. The only way good organizations can face monumental difficulties – such as trying to find their feat as the newest and youngest team in the league – is together, and by empowering staff and players alike.

"TALENT ALONE IS NEVER ENOUGH."

Despite all their early stumbles, GWS continued to develop its players into a battle-hardened, more experienced team. Everyone came together and climbed the ladder (table/standings) to an admirable fourth place finish in the 2016 and 2017 seasons.

This couldn't have happened without the coaching staff giving their players ownership. Charles van Commenee was very conscious of this concept. He knew that while many athletes were already talented, it was only taking responsibility for themselves that would enable them to fulfill their potential. Before Charles would send a program to an athlete, he'd deliberately insert in a couple of mistakes. The reasoning was two-fold: he wanted to make sure they read the program and were invested in their own training and was also soliciting feedback and suggestions about how to improve the plan. When the athlete called or emailed him and said, "I don't like this and this," he was encouraging their independence and not allowing them to be spoon fed. And the ones who noticed the errors (which, of course, they didn't know Charles had made deliberately) were often those who went on to achieve the most success.

Player empowerment is also central to the All Blacks' continued dominance. Gilbert Enoka used an analogy about the Houston Space Center to explain this. He thought of the players as Buzz Aldrin and Neil Armstrong – the ones who would have to deliver under pressure and actually walk on the moon. There were a lot of people supporting them and getting them up into space, but it was ultimately their responsibility to go out and get the final job done. For the support staff in sports, you need skilled generalists who are versatile enough to perform many tasks, just like at NASA. Gilbert also told me that just like those space race innovators, you have to make your own path, as you'll finish second (at best) if you're following someone else. He encouraged me to consider unconventional methods, as these sometimes lead to the biggest breakthroughs.

Gilbert served under the great Graham Henry. One thing that Graham, like all rugby coaches do, the day before game day is the captains' run. The fitness coach (currently Nic Gill) usually leads the warmup and then the captains of the forwards and backs take over. Sometimes the coaches are present and other times they're not, as they know they can rely on the team's senior leadership to say what needs to be said. If the coaches do attend, they say very little, if anything at all. The captains' run is the All Blacks' ritual for transferring ownership from the coaching staff to the players.

Have you found the right balance between those needed to carry the piano and play it?

COROLLARY

Leaders must lead with authority, but in great teams this never results in blind following. Clear vision must be established by the leadership, which should have all the information and be best placed to make the appropriate decisions to define the vision for the rest of the team.

APPLICATION

Great organizations face challenges together. Leaders identify the goals and vision, but they include the players and staff in the process of defining how this is achieved. The people on the ground may not have all the facts and an overall strategic view, but often have the best grasp of tactics and what's happening in the moment. Including everyone in the process creates a joint vision and joint ownership of both preparation and outcome.

"It can be quite a frustrating golf course. One of my strengths is to stay patient, and that's probably why I have performed well here in the past."

— PÁDRAIG HARRINGTON

CONFLICT BREEDS TRUST

36

All successful teams have conflict.
This breeds trust in one another.

I'm fortunate to call professor Bruce Davies a mentor. A physiologist and expert in cardiovascular physiology, cardiac disease, and hypoxia, Bruce consulted with the Welsh rugby team and many other elite organizations for decades. Bruce's knowledge was invaluable. Each morning, we conducted HRV testing long before anyone else was doing it. This provided an incredible insight into players' recovery and wellness. Bruce, Michael Graham, and Julien Baker published an incredible number of studies on a variety of topics from brain injury in boxers to the effects of dehydration to cardiovascular disease and the effects of anabolic ergogenic aids.

Julien was not just a prolific professor, but also an accomplished athlete. Quiet in demeanor, his academic abilities belied a very successful karate career. Most visitors to his home would never even notice a small photograph sitting on his mantelpiece.

The image was one we've all seen in boxing, martial arts, and MMA: the referee in the middle with one hand elevating the winner's wrist and the other holding the arm of the bloodied loser. The defeated fighter was Dolph Lundgren – best known for his role as the indomitable Ivan Drago in Rocky IV. But only on even close inspection would anyone recognize the unassuming winner, Julien Baker.

He and Bruce helped Mark Bennett, Craig White, and myself with EKG, biochemistry, and biomechanical analysis. He was a brilliant physiologist who not only contributed a lot to sporting performance, but also developed health screenings that became the gold standard in the corporate world.

"SAFE, CONSTRUCTIVE CONFLICT CAN BE THE GREATEST STIMULUS FOR PROGRESS."

The only thing Bruce loved more than his craft was a good debate. I never won. Apart from his domain expertise, I was always taken down a peg or two by his ability to make me appreciate all perspectives in an argument. He had a brilliant saying he used when he met people who were stuck in their views: "The only thing you can tell him is the time." In other words, the person wouldn't listen to or believe anyone else's view, only the time of day.

I spoke with Bruce about doing a PhD in physiology because, while I had a PhD, I hadn't obtained one in a sports-related area. But Bruce made a very good point to me, which I hadn't appreciated until then. He argued (and won, of course!) that those who often have the greatest innovative effects on teams do so because they bring expertise from outside the domain. This causes debate and conflict at first, but ultimately leads to progress.

Between Bruce, Mark, and Craig, the arguments and debates were intense, brilliant, and funny. The respect for everyone's opinion encouraged trust and honesty. There is nothing worse when you're trying to improve than no one questioning or arguing with your perspective. When the West Point performance director Justin Bokmeyer asked me to come and speak, Army head football coach Jeff Monken questioned me on the principles of *Game Changer*. When Tom Crean would visit Michigan, we debated each other on a variety of coaching-related topics. Alastair Clarkson was skeptical about the growing influence of "gurus" in sports science. All of these coaches argued their points with a genuine hunger to get better and understand more, but even when disagreements arose, they remained respectful.

Debating something exposes a healthy vulnerability, too, because you might have to accept you're wrong. This cultivates trust and only helps cement a relationship in which you can find solutions together. All of my best work has been as a result of teamwork. No one ever achieves anything meaningful alone.

Is there a culture of safe, honest, and creative conflict?

COROLLARY

Nobody enjoys working with people who are constantly argumentative for the sake of it. But there are appropriate times to debate and bring new ideas. Sometimes you need to change colleagues' perspectives, and this will occasionally lead to conflict. But you shouldn't shy away from this.

APPLICATION

The starting point for any successful conflict is to understand the other person's point of view. This allows you to prepare your counter-argument. The aim is always to find a happy conclusion for everyone, so bringing people around to your side of the debate is the goal. No matter what is said, respect must be maintained and tempers restrained. That way, trust can come from the resolution.

"Let's be the best at everything that requires no talent."

— PAUL O'CONNELL

TRAIN THEM TO LEAVE

37

Training hard is the only way to prepare for anything. Rest and recover, but never sub maximally.

Dave Buttifant is a godfather of Australian sports science and a true gentlemen. Like Neil Craig, he was an influential performance director in the AFL (Australian Football League). When I visited Collingwood Magpies, Dave asked me to present to his staff and head coach Mick Malthouse. Both he and Nathan Buckley – a Collingwood legend and soon to become head coach himself – were obviously great leaders, but what was particularly impressive was the group of people they had as a network around them.

Dave had a particularly fatherly approach to not just his role, but the field of sports science in general. He saw it as his duty to help develop students and staff to have full careers in the sport. He also had a group of advisors that contributed and consulted with the Magpies (or "Pies" as the fans call them) at that time. One was the brilliant professor Allan Hahn. He was the head of the Applied Research Centre at the Australian Institute of Sport (AIS). With a PhD in exercise physiology, Allan had a wealth of knowledge across many sports. I saw how Dave used more collaborative benchmarking and quickly adopted it. At a time when people were likely to use a very confrontational approach to improvement, Buttifant was more constructive, utilizing the expertise of people like Allan, and encouraging continuous self-improvement.

There's a great Richard Branson quote on mentorship: "Train people well enough so they can leave, treat them well enough so they don't want to." As a head coach or a business leader, it can be tempting to give into a fearful mindset that encourages you to hold back on developing other staff members because you're worried about them taking that investment to a competitor. Or perhaps, a head coach gets worried that a star assistant will take his or her job. While understandable on some levels, this is only going to harm you, them, and your organization.

"DO YOU HAVE A DEVELOPMENT PATHWAY FOR YOUR STAFF?"

While you may at some point feel that you've assembled the perfect team, you cannot preserve it forever and must instead account for the mutability of life. People move on eventually – that's just how life works. To encourage them to remain enthusiastic and do their very best now, you need to commit to continual education that helps your staff meet their goals and advance their career. Going back to Branson's quote, this creates a sense of loyalty by showing that you care. It also fulfills your responsibility to help those around you become the best possible versions of themselves. This will also have the knock-on effect of making you and the rest of the team better as everyone is constantly bringing in new and fresh ideas that prevent stagnation.

Of course, some coaches and leaders refuse to develop their people. As a result, they have very high turnover, poor retention, and weak culture. They rarely win, and certainly never achieve sustainable success.

Are you inspiring and encouraging your staff to be their best?

COROLLARY

Leaders with very high staff turnover have either poor cultures, treat team members with disdain, or have very little to offer in the way of developing people. At best these organizations float, making no progress. At worst they fail, and sometimes dramatically so.

APPLICATION

Never be afraid to develop your staff because you fear that they'll take what they've learned and leave. Inspire them to do better and always improve. It's your job to help them progress as people as well as expanding their professional skills. So create an environment they want to stay in. Always encourage them to do what's best for their well-being and happiness and that of their family.

"We have got a group of swimmers who are not just satisfied with making the team any more. They expect to win medals."

— BILL SWEETENHAM

ALWAYS MAXIMIZE YOUR STRENGTHS

38

Focus on using your strengths to defeat the opponent.

Each evening at the NFL Combine, coaches gather to catch up and share stories. I still recall having dinner in Indianapolis with various coaches from both teams and private training facilities, such as Marty Lauzon, Andy Barr, Josh Hingst, AJ Neibel, Buddy Morris, and Ian Danney. One of the most interesting people and most influential in both the NBA and NFL was Al Vermeil. One evening I sat with a number of coaches, including Rob Panariello, Derek Hansen, and Al. The great thing about this group was its relentless positivity.

You must be confident in your own knowledge and ability, but not overestimate them. Al is the only strength coach to have won rings in the NFL (with the 49ers) and the NBA (with the Chicago Bulls). When I was at Wales he'd call periodically to see how I was doing and encourage me. Al has many memorable quotes, one of which is, "The only people that made a player were his parents." Certainly, a coach can help athletes progress, learn, and develop, but they should never start to believe something like, "I made player X what she is today." That's just arrogant and also overstates the impact of the coach. Al always liked to put his role into perspective and remained humble despite reaching the pinnacle of his profession.

Anquan Boldin was a rock-hard competitor. He was both determined and mentally tough. Although he wasn't the fastest wide receiver, posting a modest 4.71 second 40 yard dash at the combine, Anquan more than compensated for this with an aggressive style of play and his incredibly smart game sense. He epitomized the word "professional" and set a standard at the San Francisco 49ers that many of his teammates aspired to reach.

"WINNERS LIMIT THEIR WEAKNESSES, BUT ALWAYS PLAY TO THEIR STRENGTHS."

Winning in sports, business, and the military requires maximizing strengths while reducing the effect of "limiting factors." I refuse to use the word "weaknesses" in this context. Elite players or world class competitors don't have weaknesses, but rather things that limit their performance. These prevent the full exploitation of other skills. For example, fast players who have underdeveloped game sense or less experience need to rely more on their speed and power to compensate. Mitigating these limiting factors makes the player more efficient and a better performer overall. To borrow a quote from Bill Knowles, "World class players are often world class compensators."

In the search for improvement, we always need to maintain our advantages and strengths. These usually determine whether we win games or not, while our limiting factors determine how much we win by. The importance of continuing to develop and maintain strengths extends to teams and organizations as much as individuals. Squads who are physical or who have great culture and spirit – such as Bolton Wanderers under Sam Allardyce – need to continue playing this way, but must also reduce the impact of their limiting factors, such as lesser talent. They can compensate by using tactical formations or strategies.

Sometimes our strengths are not directly sports-related, but are personality driven. Many of the best players are those who have the greatest attention to detail. One example is tennis legend Ivan Lendl. He explained to me how he would prepare for major championships like Wimbledon and the US Open by replicating the playing surface at his home court. He'd use the company (and same exact work crew) that installed the court at the tournament venue to make sure it played the same way. The result? Eight Grand Slam titles.

Do you have a healthy emphasis on both maintaining your strengths and mitigating the effects of limiting factors?

COROLLARY

Limiting factors can be improved and their negative affect on performance reduced. The best athletes mitigate their limitations. Strengths can compensate and be maximized, so improve both at the same time.

APPLICATION

Your strengths are what help you win. Your limitations determine by how much. But unless your strengths are constantly practiced at the highest intensity possible, they will deteriorate.

"I'm driven by passion, not by anger. What drives me is the passion to expose and correct what is wrong with the sport. That is the passion. That's mistaken for anger because I get, clearly, worked up about it. But it's not anger. So yeah...I make it very easy for them, because you can mistake passion for anger. They ain't the same things."

— PAUL KIMMAGE

INNOVATION, RESILIENCE, & KNOWLEDGE

EAT SOUP WITH A KNIFE

39

The ability to adapt determines
your ability to succeed. Be formless.

In a small American frontier town in the early 1830s, a crowded bar buzzed with heated debate. Men from all backgrounds were gathered around shouting and arguing. The more the beer flowed, the louder voices grew. The argument was over the finer points of bow and arrow construction.

One group argued about the best choice of wood for the shaft, while another quibbled over the style of tip. Others were in a heated debate over the type of feathers that were best suited to straightest and fastest arrow flight. As tempers flared and faces grew redder, no one noticed a man in the corner of the bar sitting quietly on his own. Under a flickering lamp he sketched and etched a design. Pausing only occasionally to sip his drink, the quiet stranger ignored the loud voices around him. As the night drew to a close, he had finished his beer – and the first draft of a hand pistol.

Samuel Colt walked out into the crisp winter air.

Charlie Francis told me that story in his living room. Of course, this is not the true story of how the handgun was invented, but Charlie used the anecdote to make a point: while others argue about the seemingly obvious and quibble over details, start looking beyond incremental improvements and think bigger.

The term "eat soup with a knife" comes from a book I read many years ago by Lieutenant Colonel John A. Nagl. He wrote it at a juncture when there was a terrible realization in the military community that conventional warfare had changed. A veteran of both Operation Desert Storm and the Iraq War, Nagl wrote about counterinsurgency lessons from the Malayan Emergency conflicts from 1948 to 1960 and in Vietnam from 1950 to 1975. In modern conflict, the enemy and method has been constantly changing at a great speed that, until recently, outpaced our ability to understand these changes and adapt to them. This is the same challenge sports and sports science are now facing.

"THE GREATEST ABILITY IS ADAPTABILITY."

The New Zealand All Blacks have been at the pinnacle of team sports success for many years. Everyone in a group environment knows who they are and tries to emulate them. If you're going to learn, why not learn from the best? Coincidently, as I was reading more and more about training and coaching teams, the name of one strength coach kept coming up time and time again. Ashley Jones was the strength coach for the All Blacks. Along with Graham Lowe, who helped define the roll of sports director, Ashley was responsible for their physical preparation.

An impressive thing about Ashley is his openness to new approaches and methods. Though he was at the pinnacle of the profession, he certainly didn't think he knew everything, and was actually eager to learn from me about Gaelic football. Ashley had the All Blacks play small-sided games with Aussie rules footballs and the Gaelic footballs I'd brought, believing that the different sizes and shapes would challenge the players' skills. Sometimes they'd allow forward passes even though you can't do that in rugby, to get used to catching the ball from different angles. The team would also play soccer, which would help keep things fresh and prevent rugby from becoming a chore. Ashley also adapted children's games like "rats and rabbits," in which the players would run to various circles placed around the field and put balls in them. This was the first time I'd seen a coach use small-sided games in such a diverse and creative way.

The thing I didn't initially understand was how a highly skilled team could learn from playing "without" the rules. Wouldn't participating in games that were contrary to the regulations in rugby negatively affect the players who'd been honing specific skill sets for years? Wouldn't forward passes, round balls, and different bounces have a deleterious impact? It went against everything I'd read academically about skill development.

But the lesson became apparent to me. Ashley was teaching the players adaptability and developing their decision-making skills under duress by taking them out of their comfort zone. The unorthodox games also helped improve and stretch their peripheral vision. It was done in context and never over emphasized to the point where it became an issue.

Another "aha" moment concerning adaptability came when Henk Kraaijenhof shared with me the concept of the Omega Paradox. Years later, along with another young coach Gerrit Keferstein, I saw this phenomenon more and more. This paradox stipulates that when learning you go in a straight line for a while, then around in a semi-circle learning new ideas, and finally back to another straight line that's close to where you began. In coaching, this could mean that you'd start off with a simple approach, then go off and learn more about biomechanics or some other discipline. Once you'd immersed yourself in deep learning in this new area, you'd come back to coaching in a very similar manner to before, but with a new understanding and perspective that would benefit both you and, more importantly, your players.

Vitor Frade is the pioneer of tactical periodization, but this alone doesn't summarize his influence on soccer and team sports. Frade developed players who could adapt. Like Carlos Queiroz and others, Frade understands that you have to provide athletes with problem solving-based learning experiences and principles that respect the laws of sociology and biology. And to keep them progressing throughout their careers, they must be exposed to new learning opportunities.

In any walk of life, you must adapt to change and embrace it. Don't try to always preserve the status quo.

Have you developed the ability to adapt, grow, and change?

COROLLARY

While you must adapt, two common mistakes many people make are changing for the sake of it and abandoning their principles. You must identify your values, remain principled, and create a methodology that rarely changes, while altering tactics when needed.

APPLICATION

Accept that success is the ability to adapt to unforeseen circumstances. Learn to enjoy challenges. Accept them! Look for fun ways to think outside the box. Some of the best ideas will come from encouraging this growth mindset.

"I always try to remember that praise and a slap on your back is only six inches away from a kick up the arse!"

– ANTHONY "AXEL" FOLEY

NO DIFFERENCE BETWEEN WINNING OR LOSING

Lesson

40

How to manage emotion.

Though now regarded as one of the most influential coaches in British rugby league history, Tony Smith lost his first 15 games. Would you have had the resilience to keep going if that was you?

Tony demonstrated to me the importance of finding victory in any situation. He was mentally tough but gained this resilience by understanding his vulnerability. He focused on progress, not perfection. Tony always kept perspective, no matter how well or poorly his team was doing. He will tell you to this day that losing those initial games taught him how to handle both wins and losses with the same attitude. I've learned a lot from him.

His head coaching career started at Huddersfield Giants when he took over a team that was in the midst of a losing streak and about to be relegated to the league below.

They lost the last three games of that season and failed to avoid the dreaded drop. The following year the Giants lost the first 12 games, until finally they tied one and started turning things around.

Fortunately, the owner kept faith with Tony and the team soon got back to its winning ways. Tony was very philosophical about these trials and soon came to see each setback as a learning opportunity for himself and his team. Even when the squad was underperforming, he'd find positives for the group as a whole and for each player. Tony identified just one or two things for every individual to work on after a win or loss. This was very helpful, as athletes can easily let their heads drop when they're not playing at their best or be overwhelmed by a coach demanding that they improve at everything all at once.

The benefit of Tony's "turn a negative into a positive" method was that his players started to regain confidence in their abilities, even though the team had to endure a few more losses. They also valued that Tony was watching everything they did and looking for ways to help them and the team improve. In elite sports your only true opponent is yourself. The same principle applies when you're thriving: find the small wins.

"ATTACK WINS AND LOSSES WITH THE SAME RUTHLESSNESS."

Against an overwhelming favorite who you think you've got no chance of beating, you should focus on what you can do well and that determines your definition of a win, regardless of the scoreboard. Sometimes the result might even surprise you – which is why competitions like the FA Cup in soccer and March Madness in basketball are so compelling.

Even if you don't pull off an upset, you can focus on what went your way – again redefining what you mean by a "win." Immediately after a game, coaches often have a "hot wash," which is a quick review or sitrep (situation report). They follow this up with an AAR (After Action Review), usually that night or the next morning.

The best leaders recognize wins and losses, celebrate or mourn them for a while, and then move resolutely on. They never get too emotional either way, instead pouring their energy into attacking the sitrep and AAR and responding to victory and defeat with equal ruthlessness.

How do you manage the highs and lows of the business, the wins, and the losses?

COROLLARY

In extreme situations you have to compare yourself to only yourself. On one level, the scoreboard is all that matters, but you can still find positives in defeat. You should also ensure that the targets or KPIs (Key Performance Indicators) you set for the players are aligned with the game model and game plan.

APPLICATION

Determine your opponent's ability. Be brave and ambitious. Win or lose, learn from it, and use the result to improve regardless. Also remember to aim big and assess small.

"If I carried all that sort of stuff on my shoulders going into a game, I wouldn't be able to get out there."

— TANA UMAGA

THREE IS THE MAGIC NUMBER

Lesson

41

**Only give people three things to do at any time.
Three rules, three things to remember.**

I was a little confused and demoralized. I'd spent many hours creating kicking drills for the Welsh rugby team and packaged them in a beautifully designed manual for Neil Jenkins. He was the Wales kicking coach and a legend in his own right. "Jenks" was the first player to score 1,000 points in international matches – a true great of the game. We'd been having issues with both our kicking and catching high balls. With my experience in Gaelic football and Aussie rules football (AFL), I'd put together a manual of drills and games to help improve these areas and given it to Neil. But after a few weeks, I'd not seen him open or use it.

Then one afternoon Neil popped his head around my office door and shouted, "Hey Fergie boy, let's go!" I followed him. "Come on son," he called back over his shoulder as he headed for the indoor practice field called "The Barn" with a ball in his hand.

"Ok Fergie son, let's go through the 'over the water kicking game' you drew in that book."

For the next hour and a half, I ran through drills in The Barn with Wales's highest ever points-scorer and the third highest of all-time in international rugby using a soft rugby ball and scattered cones.

That night I asked Jenks if the diagrams weren't clear enough.

"No, they were fine son, but I need to do drills to understand them," he replied.

The obvious lesson was that learning is different for everyone, coaches and players alike. Neil was a rugby legend. He had an incredibly well-developed kinesthetic sense, both in learning and teaching. This was why he was not only a great kicker, but also a fantastic coach.

At Wales rugby and the San Francisco 49ers, I picked up a lot of valuable experience in learning styles. Sometimes as coaches we can get too fixated on our preferred way of teaching something and become set in our ways. But we know from educational research that people learn differently, and this isn't limited to school classrooms.

"ALWAYS FOCUS ON THE LEARNING EXPERIENCE, NOT JUST THE TEACHING INPUT."

For shy players in the Welsh squad, we'd get them to sing or give a short speech to bring them out of their shells. Others learned by listening. That day I found out that Neil Jenkins was more of a kinesthetic learner. Giving him a book of kicking drills meant nothing to him. Going down to the field and actually doing each drill with him was far more effective.

From then on, I realized learning among elite performers was far more complex than just drawing plays and expecting people to learn them. So I began studying everything I could, from subliminal messages to advertising, to learn more about different ways of transmitting ideas.

I've always said, "Sports science doesn't give you answers, it just allows you to ask better questions," and Neil's example backed this up. My question was simple: how do I communicate and teach players effectively?

I learned that a big part of successful communication is in how you package things and how impactful it can be to use slogans, rhymes, imagery, parables, and metaphors. One guideline I began using was "the rule of three." I drafted short presentations with no more than three points, three reasons, or three rules. This is about all a player can retain and act upon. We see a similar communication strategy in TED Talks, which are often centered on a single big idea and have garnered a massive worldwide audience because of their simplicity and clarity.

World renowned strength coach Charles Poliquin taught me something very important about communication. He repeatedly said that most people want a simple formula for everything: A+B=C. I think about that every time I present to a group – how can I clarify my message and break it down into a series of easy, adaptable takeaways that people will remember? Solutions to human performance are always complex, but people want them conveyed in straightforward ways that they can understand and apply.

Simple but effective teaching doesn't just have to come from experienced veterans with decades of experience. Back in the late 90s I went to a conference in the middle of Ireland at an isolated community hall to hear a 20-something-year-old American speak about shoulder and ankle rehab. I initially thought this baby-faced Bostonian was either lost or someone had fooled him into being there, but he went on to give a profound presentation. Eric Cressey certainly knew his area very well, but the key was how he presented the information in a way that could be understood by the audience in front of him.

What would you take away from your advertising campaigns or speeches if you were the one listening to them?

COROLLARY

There are times when there's a lot of information to be disseminated. How this is presented is critical to your team's ability to retain it. Careful presentation of the information leads to retention and an ability to apply what you've taught.

APPLICATION

Break information into chunks. Be cognizant of your audience and who the information is being delivered to. Just because you know the material doesn't mean your audience will. It doesn't matter what you know. All that matters is what they do after you're finished speaking to them.

"107 caps isn't bad for someone who isn't 'a top, top player,' is it? I never expected to get that amount of caps. When I made my debut, I set myself the personal target of trying to get 50 caps and score 10 goals if I could. So to have 107 is something I am really proud of."

— STEVEN GERRARD

THE OPERATION WAS A SUCCESS, BUT THE PATIENT DIED

Lesson

42

What is a win?

With the explosion of interest in analytics following the bestseller list and box office success of *Moneyball*, many sports teams tried to emulate the Oakland A's. Yet few truly understood the origin of Bill James's methods. At the Welsh rugby team, any attempt at quantitative measurement was handled by the analysis department. The goal of the team at that time was to prepare the fittest squad possible to win and Craig White masterminded this to great effect.

After every game, the video analysis guys would go straight back to the hotel and work through the night fueled by coffee and Red Bull, analyzing film and cutting it so that the next morning as the coaches and players came down for breakfast, reports would be ready and film would be organized.

Around this time, they identified one statistic that was common to all wins: ball-in-play time. A rugby game is 80 minutes long. But when stoppages and breaks are accounted for, the actual playing time can be as low as 32 minutes. According to the video guys, when we kept the ball in play for over 34 minutes, we won 98% of our games. In other words, no team could live with our level of fitness.

So the emphasis on fitness and especially on strength, power, and anaerobic conditioning became even more pronounced. We stepped up training and spared no expense. We invested in force platforms, GPS units, and sports science. Results appeared to prove we were on the correct path. We beat Australia in a memorable and very physical game at the Millennium Stadium in which the ball was in play for 34 minutes. Our biggest test would come against the All Blacks, again at home in Cardiff.

No one prepares for any opponent like they prepare to play New Zealand. It's the greatest test of where you are as a team. We made sure the players were ready. The tension was obvious before the game even started. In a now-famous incident, the Welsh players stood in a line facing the All Blacks' intimidating Haka war dance, but when it was over they refused to move, continuing to stare their opponents down. The Welsh players were making a statement that they would not move until the All Blacks broke.

"WHAT IS A WIN?"

Neither side budged.

Both teams continued to glare at each other. The referee Jonathan Kaplan was growing impatient. He blew the whistle to try and get them to disperse and start the game, but still neither side would budge. Seconds ticked by. The tension was electric and the crowd was growing excited. Kaplan began to sense that the scenario could easily get out of control. He walked to both captains and asked them to break up their groups. But Ryan Jones and Richie McCaw both told him they would only move when the other team did. As the clock now ticked past 90 seconds, two groups of huge men stood in the middle of the field just eyeballing each other. Eventually, the All Blacks, accepting that the Welsh had made their point, broke up slowly and the game got under way.

This was a good Welsh team, the grand-slam champions of the Six Nations who were aiming for their first win over New Zealand in 55 years. We started at a ferocious pace, went on the attack, and hit the New Zealanders with everything we had. The All Blacks struggled at first with the physical intensity and we kept the ball in play as high up the pitch as we could. We earned a penalty in the first minute and Stephen Jones landed the kick. But eventually the All Blacks found their rhythm. On the back foot, we gave away a penalty. The scores were level within seconds through Dan Carter's boot. What slowly became apparent was that the All Blacks were adjusting. They weren't trying to beat us at our own game, but rather were allowing us possession and forcing us into making errors. In the end, we only scored three penalties. We never penetrated the All Blacks defense at all and didn't score a try, while they ran in two tries and kicked five penalties.

The game ended 29-9 to the All Blacks.

Two days later as I was walking through the building – which had all the atmosphere of a funeral home – I passed one of the video analysts. As he walked by a thought crossed my mind. I turned and called back to him, "Do you know what the ball in play time was?"

"36 minutes."

The operation was a success, but the patient died. We had played at a greater intensity than ever before, but we lost the game. Force platforms, GPS units, and sports science made no difference to winning a game against the best team in world rugby.

There are a few lessons to take from this.

First, fitness and sports science have a limited influence on performance. Analytics can only tell you so much. In fact, if you believe a tech toy is an important factor in winning a complex team sport game, I have a leprechaun who wants to sell you a magic castle in Ireland. Looking at only one factor in isolation is myopic.

Second, winning games at the top level is not about what you do well, it's about making as few mistakes as possible. The best teams force you into errors and capitalize on them. It's all about discipline. Winning is a complex, intricate problem to be solved.

Finally, the only metric that really matters in the end is the game score. All analytics and KPIs must be developed in a constantly evolving matrix that directly leads to the scoreboard changing for the better.

Bill Sweetenham was a firm believer in winning at all costs, as long as you stayed within the rules. He understood that you couldn't always put in an optimal performance on game day, but even when this eluded you, you must still find a way to get the victory. There's also a time to define a win as something different. Goals must be ambitious, but realistic. A young team that loses 2-1 to the league leader might consider this a victory in terms of the players coming together and battling hard until the very end. As long as there's a game-to-game improvement, you're on the right track.

Ivan Lendl once told me that a loss is only an issue when you don't learn from it. He hated losing more than he craved winning and remembered all of his defeats in great detail. He was driven by his failures and believed that good preparation could help a player overcome a lot of psychological challenges.

And skill can help you surmount a lot of physical ones. During my time at Bolton Wanderers, I saw the crucial importance of skill in sports. I was laying cones on one of my first days before practice began and the players were warming up. Prolific striker Nicolas Anelka strolled out of the changing rooms. Veteran defender Ricardo Gardner kicked a ball from over 50 yards away toward Nicolas. Anelka was still pulling his training shirt over his head. Without breaking stride, he put out his left foot and stopped the ball dead beneath him while barely looking at it. I was astonished by his skill level – not just Gardner's pinpoint cross-field pass, but also Anelka's ability to casually make the ball obey his will even as he was still getting changed.

Up until that point, most of what I'd heard in strength and conditioning circles was about the need for more speed, power, and endurance. While these things are obviously significant, it wasn't until I saw Anelka in action that I realized how skill often trumps all other physical qualities. This was the most dangerous striker in the Premier League. He was lightning fast, very skillful, driven, and athletic, but nowhere close to the most powerful. The technical aspect of the game can be even more impactful, and can also enable players who aren't the biggest, strongest, or fastest to be successful, even at the highest level. This not only made me reevaluate how I thought about soccer, but also rugby and other sports where I'd always considered the most physically dominating players to be the best.

Watching Justin Smith at the San Francisco 49ers typified another mistake people watching team sports often make. Yes, Justin was probably the strongest player on the team, but his functional strength was maximized by his skill, not the other way around. People often don't appreciate the skill element that's always present in demonstrations of strength. Strength is a skill. And Justin was both skillful and strong.

Are you putting analytics in the proper context, or letting the numbers run your organization?

COROLLARY

Few companies can operate on human instinct alone. The world we function in now has more data than ever before. Harnessing and using science and modern analytics can help in very useful and practical ways, but only when put into context and applied with common sense.

APPLICATION

Science and analytics are the dashboard of your car. They provide signals and indications – confirmations if you will – that what you are doing is correct. They are necessary, but only after the basic model is in place. To quote Bill Sweetenham, "Science should be on tap, not on top."

"In this world, you can choose to be positive, or you can choose to be negative. You can choose to see things through a set of eyes that sees good, or you can choose to see things in life that aren't so good."

— JACK HARBAUGH

HENRY'S HORSE

43

**Innovate and think outside the box
to constantly improve.**

If you were playing for the Welsh rugby team in 2008, you arrived for breakfast each morning at a dining hall reserved for the team in the lower level of the Vale of Glamorgan Hotel. Stripping down to your shorts, you'd stand on a scale and answer eight short questions on a connected touch-screen tablet. Then you'd pull on your tracksuit again and go to eat with your teammates.

The scales automatically registered your weight and also measured bio-impedance (an indicator of resistance to an imperceptible current). Your answers to questions about sleep quality, mood, stiffness, and soreness were compared to your norms for that day and delivered to those who needed it immediately. The strength staff knew who to refer to nutritionists for dehydration, medical staff for injury, and psychologists for mood, etc. All of this was based on a system that I had designed and built using input from people as diverse as McLaren Formula 1 team members and experts in sales and marketing at Google.

Remember, this was over 10 years ago, long before anyone else had heard of athlete management platforms. I stopped using such systems after a number of years, as athletes evolved and I identified the optimal way to use technology. For example, with younger athletes there was a resistance to invasive monitoring. With older players, we discovered that simple conversations revealed much more information and built trust. In some cases, I've found that overreliance on technology actually makes us less focused on the actual player as a person. We miss out on small yet important details concerning their life that no metrics can quantify.

I was on a constant search to evolve and innovate, but only with the singular goal of improving performance. If it didn't work, we got rid of it. Then there was the issue of data analysis. Often, we struggled to properly analyze the data in a way that noticed real issues. We found most statistical methods unreliable for the nature and volume of information we had. I soon found out that we were never going to be able to gather enough accurate data on a player to have the benefits of institutions like Facebook or Google where big data was key to analysis.

One analytics expert at Facebook told me he found out fast that small data sets from one person were essentially useless. They needed larger data sets and more data points to produce analysis or predictions of any validity. Analyzing averages was pointless. For several years I made the incorrect assumption that technology meant innovation. As time went by, I realized that true innovation was about improvement on the complete spectrum, from ergonomics to culture to human-machine interfacing.

"INNOVATION IS A MINDSET, NOT A SITUATION."

Eddie Jones, the current England rugby coach, was someone who demonstrated this to great effect. I was introduced to him by Australian fitness coach Dean Benton and was immediately struck by what a progressive thinker Eddie was, which was no surprise as that sums Dean up too. I'd send him emails early in the morning and Eddie would reply within minutes, even though it was the middle of the night in Australia. He was always looking for new ways to find an edge. Eddie brought in Australian Rules coaches to upskill the squad in catching and psychologists to speak to his staff about mental wellness. He recognized that there was a lot to learn from non-rugby sources, and such open-mindedness helped him create a refreshing way to coach the England squad. It also helps keep things interesting for the players and encourages them to broaden their thinking. You need outside ideas and to consider what others in your area are not thinking about. To quote Henry Ford, "If I had asked people what they wanted, they would have said faster horses."

I also began to notice that the most innovative coaches all appeared to have one other thing in common: most of them worked with teams and organizations with limited resources. When I first met Eddie, he was with the Japanese national rugby team. His head of fitness John Pryor (JP) was an ingenious coach, and with Japan, he was able to squeeze maximum results from a virtually non-existent budget. JP had to be incredibly inventive and creative.

Rather than having a world-class gym like most national teams, they'd use low cost equipment like sand bags and bands to prepare the players. He was able to apply everything he knew in a restricted environment to get results.

This paradoxically appeared to have two effects – a more positive training environment and more adaptable players. Most of all, complacency was never a problem. Working with other teams where budgets were unlimited, I found the answer to an issue always seemed to be money-related, rather than true problem solving. The trouble is, that's rarely the answer. Eddie Jones did an exceptional job with that team, sowing the seeds that eventually saw them defeat South Africa at the 2015 Rugby World Cup in one of the sport's biggest upsets. Eddie's staff showed how to be creative on a low budget while with him in Japan.

I also came to realize that you need to be on the lookout for opportunities to learn from unexpected sources. Many years ago while studying for my PhD, I was lodging in the postgrad student dorm during the summer. There were very few people around, but a visiting expert was staying in my building for a few days. One evening he came into the common area while I was watching TV and introduced himself as Giannandrea Poesio.

At the time Giannandrea was a dance correspondent for the *Guardian* newspaper in London and was visiting the University of Limerick to teach. He had been an understudy to the legendary Rudolf Nureyev and led a fascinating life. Giannandrea helped choreograph movie scenes and had stories about so many performers, from James Stewart to Dolph Lundgren (yes, another Ivan Drago anecdote). He taught me that if you want to be the best, you have to apprentice with the best. My conversations with Giannandrea left a lasting impression – you can learn something of value from anyone in any domain. It was here I first started to formulate concepts in *Game Changer*. You can't cocoon yourself inside your comfort zone. A wise man can learn from a fool, but a fool cannot learn from a wise man.

Of course, you can innovate and learn from within the sporting community as well. Dan Pfaff helped me understand running and movement not just within track events, but also in the context of team sports. He has a unique way of troubleshooting athletes' issues. An excessive amount of lateral movement, for example, might involve a myriad of contributing factors, from muscle activation and mobility to quadratus lumborum dysfunction. Dan's thorough understanding of anatomy, ability to listen to his athletes, and technical know-how are all world class. Even in areas related to recovery, Dan was investigating certain therapies decades before anyone else.

A lot of coaches I've encountered rely heavily on strength training, while others emphasize technique above all. Dan masterfully balanced both. He never thought he had definitive answers, but would say, "I think this is what's going on. What about you?" Instead of professing to be an authority on everything, Dan would lean on other experts in various domains, learn from them, and incorporate their best practices into his own coaching.

How innovative is your staff? Are you leading or following the herd?

COROLLARY

A critical yet often overlooked aspect of adaptation and survival in both business and sports is innovation. But innovation without reason or for its own sake can be detrimental to progress. Not everything will work, and it's foolish to equate each new technology with progress. You must be sure implementation will deliver results and not just create unnecessary work and greater complexity.

APPLICATION

Ingenuity can come from many sources. Occasionally you will be inspired by ideas from completely outside your realm. Much innovation comes from necessity. Very often those working with limited budgets are the most creative thinkers.

"I realized that the past failures had strengthened me, taught me that no one is immune from mistakes. True leaders must learn from their failures, use the lessons to motivate themselves, and not be afraid to try again or make the next tough decision."

— ADMIRAL WILLIAM H. MCRAVEN

THE TOMATO FRUIT SALAD

44

Know the difference between intelligence/ knowledge and data.

Craig White was the head fitness coach at Wasps rugby team in London and when he moved to Leicester Tigers, he asked me to visit with new nutritional protocols that would limit the negative effects of inflammation and speed up player recovery. Craig had coached with Warren Gatland at Wasps and they'd enjoyed a lot of success together, winning every trophy available.

One reason that Craig had such an impact on the large squad at Leicester was because he utilized his assistant coaches, many of whom were interns. Though they were young, he gave them a lot of responsibility and wanted them to learn on the job doing meaningful work with the team, rather than just performing menial tasks. As a result, the entire team got stronger and fitter. Craig was also one of the first strength coaches to utilize pre- and post-workout shakes, years before they became commonplace. He knew more about nutrition than just about anyone.

Craig introduced a new way of training the bigger, more powerful players like the props. Most coaches at the time had everyone running a lot, but Craig saw that this was making it hard for the big guys to preserve their muscle mass. So he developed their aerobic capacity through weight training and only had them run the bare minimum needed to maintain their match fitness. He also had them do wrestling drills, which helped with their coordination, balance, and applying power from odd angles and positions.

"NEVER CONFUSE INFORMATION WITH WISDOM."

At one point the squad was struggling with a lot of nagging ligament and tendon injuries, which was preventing full practice. Many of the younger academy players had poor eating habits. Over dinner that evening with the team doctor, Craig asked what I'd recommend. I thought for a while and then suggested a simple solution: Craig should provide breakfast for the players each morning. Not the high carb kind they'd probably eat at home, but one that consisted of chicken, meat, turkey, fish, and vegetables. The doctor disagreed, but I explained that this would ensure every member of the squad would start the day with a good meal that was high in fat and protein and would carry them through morning training.

Soon enough, Leicester Tigers were providing breakfast and other meals for the squad. Players started eating breakfast as a group, which improved comradery. Getting everyone together first thing also gave coaches and staff the chance to check how fully they'd recovered from the previous day's session and encouraged them to come in early enough to get treatment. Young players who hadn't developed good eating habits were exposed to the standard Craig expected of them. The results were profound. While the new meal plan increased costs, the benefits were evident not just in improved nutrition, but also in player welfare, health, and fitness. Often the simplest solution is the best one.

When we worked together at the Welsh rugby team years later, Craig and I had to improve to compete with other teams, especially the Southern Hemisphere squads. We decided to invest in GPS to try and enhance the players' physical performance. I told Warren Gatland that I'd like to purchase 30 units for the team. He thought about it for a moment and asked, "Would it be better if we got 40 so there's one for every player?" That was rare, as many coaches would have refused such an expensive proposal. Slightly stunned and not wanting to waste the opportunity, I quickly said, "Yes, thank you." Then I reminded him that I didn't have enough in my budget for 40 GPS units. "Don't worry, I'll take it out of my personal budget," he said. As a result, we became one of the first rugby teams to experiment with GPS.

Dave Buttifant had an approach that took every aspect of his athletes' physical and mental states into account. Like Craig, he was a great mentor to me and other young coaches coming up through the ranks. Dave had acquired incredible wisdom and created unique and highly effective ways to benchmark, evaluate, and develop coaching staff. He was as considerate as he was talented. Dave knew that to perpetuate knowledge in any field you have to pass it on and be open about everything you've learned over the years, so others can benefit from and add to it.

Kelly Starrett is another great teacher who oozes charisma. A great friend of mine, Kelly is a CrossFit coach and physical therapist. His 2013 book *Becoming a Supple Leopard* was featured on *The New York Times* bestseller list for months. Along with his wife Juliet, Kelly shares his movement and mobility principles via his website, mobilityWOD.com. Behind this Supple Leopard is an incredible wealth of knowledge of not just human anatomy, but also functional anatomy and physiology. Kelly has many skills, yet his ability to distill information into something useful and transferrable is unique in human performance.

In today's world we have plenty of data and lots of information. This isn't where true value lies, but rather in knowledge and cultivating wisdom through experience. As the British journalist, musician, and broadcaster Miles Kington once said, "Knowledge is knowing that a tomato is a fruit, wisdom is not putting it in a fruit salad."

Are you balancing wisdom with youth and enthusiasm in the most appropriate way to achieve lasting success?

COROLLARY

Experimentation and innovation are important, but ultimately there is no replacement for knowledge. Experience provides wisdom, learned from making mistakes and watching others do the same.

APPLICATION

In business, the ability of teams to tolerate all perspectives brings with it the energy and innovation of some and the learning and experiences of others, but all of these must be underpinned by fundamental understanding. Data and information need to be interpreted and converted to actionable knowledge.

"The only people that made a player were his parents."

— AL VERMEIL

BURN THE BOATS

45

Move on from bad experiences. Don't cling to past victories either.

Sir Clive Woodward, coach of the last English rugby team to win the Rugby World Cup, sat across the board room table, the sun beaming in through the early morning London smog. He asked me what the coaching staff did at the various teams I'd been with when we won or lost games. When someone like Sir Clive puts you on the spot, you swallow hard.

After trying to think how he was trying to catch me out, I said, "Well if we win, we usually either go home or go out and celebrate as a team. If we lose, depending on the time the game ends, we go right back to the office or come in early the next day."

"Exactly!" Sir Clive replied. "When we win, players all go out and get drunk and celebrate. But when we lose, we bring them in the next morning and start over-analyzing our mistakes."

One of the greatest lessons Sir Clive taught me was so simple and clear that I felt embarrassed I hadn't thought of it before. Rather than over-emphasizing the great things we do in games when we play well, ingraining positive habits in players, and building their confidence, we do the opposite and rehash the mistakes to death. Sir Clive also said that sometimes there are games in which things just go wrong and you need to let players walk away and clear their heads.

"KNOW WHEN TO WALK AWAY AND WHEN TO WALK ON."

You also have to face adverse circumstances head on. In 1519, Captain Hernán Cortés landed on a new and unfamiliar coastline, with 600 Spanish soldiers, 16 horses, and 11 boats. He had arrived in Veracruz in Mexico with no idea what lay ahead, but he imagined vast treasures. However, grumbling began among his men who, like Cortés, knew that other conquistadors with far more resources had attempted this journey and perished.

Legend has it that Cortés stood on the beaches and with a deeply passionate speech, inspired his troops. He ended his pre-conquest pep talk with three, now famous, words that would change the world as we know it: "Burn the boats." Because they had no chance of turning around and sailing home, his men knew they must fight through adversity, come what may.

Fast forward almost 500 years and I was sitting in San Francisco thinking about Cortés and his boat burning. I think the day I left the team, Keena Turner celebrated because he had never been interrogated by anyone like me, who peppered him with question after question. But none-theless, he was kind and generous with his time. Keena was a wealth of knowledge about what made Ronnie Lott, Joe Montana, Steve Young, Jerry Rice, and Bill Walsh tick, what motivated them, and how they succeeded.

One day I asked for Keena's advice. I was worried that I was failing to get my message across to the team. He looked me right in the eye and said, "You don't give your-self enough credit. You're having a bigger impact on these guys than you realize. I know because they've told me you're appreciated here." Then he left me with an indeli-ble phrase: "You're a lion and lions never worry about the opinions of sheep."

When things get difficult, don't doubt yourself. Don't concern yourself with the opinions of sheep or those who are not at your standard or level. If you've made a bad mis-take, burn your boats, believe in yourself, and attack. As José Mourinho once said about ignoring critics so you can focus on your mission, "You will never reach your destina-tion if you stop and throw stones at every dog that barks." Are you invested in learning from your mistakes?

COROLLARY

We learn from failure, but we should also learn from success. Remove emotion from the situation and look calmly and objectively at reality.

APPLICATION

We need to have faith in what we know to be true. Sometimes we overanalyze when things appear to be bad, and we don't give ourselves credit when things are actually very good. Instead of letting outside doubters and our own fears derail us, we need to burn the boats, ignore a bad performance, and look for the positives in what we have achieved. Wallowing in self-pity won't achieve anything. And no matter what the result is, you have no way to go but forward.

"Most people have reliable partners and sharing with a partner is one of the joys of life. However, basing your security on a partner or any other one individual is a recipe for disaster."

— STEVE PETERS

YOU DON'T KNOW
WHAT YOU DON'T KNOW

46

Trust what you know to be true. Don't second guess yourself, but neither believe you know everything.

Imagine this scenario.

It's the day before a big game. The coaching war room is packed. This meeting should be quick and seamless. The head coach has just entered the room and sits down at the head of the table, with his coaching staff on one side and the performance team on the other. The medical director sits nearest the head coach and the strength coach is seated at the opposite end of the table. Assistants are lined up leaning against the wall, notepads in hand, chewing on the ends of their pencils. Sheets of paper for the planned training session are being handed out. The sports scientist is in the corner of the room with his laptop on his knees. The head coach outlines the plan for the day and turns to the head of medical.

"Who's in or out for today? How's Jonny doing?"

"Well, Jonny [the team MVP] blew out his hamstring at the end of practice and he's going to be out for six weeks."

From the corner of the room comes an ecstatic, "Yes!" The sports scientist leaps excitedly from his chair and punches the air in triumph. "My injury prediction model works!"

That is *never* going to happen. While this scenario is obviously exaggerated, some people in the sports science field are looking at so-called "injury prevention" in entirely the wrong way.

"THE MORE YOU LEARN, THE MORE YOU REALIZE HOW LITTLE YOU DON'T REALLY KNOW."

At Wales, the British and Irish Lions, and Liverpool, I had developed quite a comprehensive computer system for tracking injuries and mood scores using combinations of GPS data, touchscreen monitoring, and HRV testing, among other things. Relying on my PhD and understanding of technology, I was able to integrate, analyze, and build heuristics that not only collected data, but also empowered my colleagues to put it to good use.

At the time, the insight was driven by sabermetrics. I'd learned from Dan Pfaff, Charlie Francis, and Henk Kraaijenhof that to really improve you need to go to the source, so I immersed myself not in *Moneyball*, but in Bill James's original writings and the books he'd used to come up with his unique approach to metric-based analysis. I then applied these lessons with a concrete focus on turning the data into actionables and deliverables.

I adopted a very simple approach that I still believe in. Any non-contact soft tissue injury in team sports is unacceptable. We know so much about this type of injury that we should be able to eliminate them. I then went one step further: to me, even a non-contact ACL injury or ankle ligament injury should be avoidable.

I firmly believed that with all of the data we were gathering, we should have been able to develop algorithms to predict injury. I traveled around Europe to learn from statisticians who were only too happy to help. With the assistance of professors at the University of Salford and other top colleges, I built probability models that demonstrated how we could predict the likelihood of these injuries occurring and how the probability changed depending on proximity to the event.

But something slowly dawned on me: I didn't know what I didn't know. I slowly realized that I'd never have full access or the possibility of gathering all the data I needed to create the injury prediction model I'd dreamed of. And if there was any chance of injury, we'd be forced to intervene or add prehabilitation protocols to the training program. In teams sports you can never prove you're truly able to predict injury with anywhere close to 100% accuracy – though that doesn't mean you aren't preventing them.

First of all, while I had more data from our teams than anyone else, I never had it all. Secondly, the training programs changed so much that the environment was constantly shifting and so too the inputs. But most importantly, I would never be able to prove I was right.

Charles Poliquin believed that you can maintain and even improve aerobic conditioning through strength training, which influenced the coaching of Craig White and many others. Charles was a voracious reader who drew from any and every field as he continued to evolve his beliefs and practices. The same goes for Paul Chek and Louie

Simmons, both of whom have had a massive impact on performance optimization worldwide.

Frans Bosch was another influential sprint coach I took a lot from. Much of it came from our disagreements about various techniques and methods. He was a formidable debater and could hold his own on just about any aspect of performance. When we butted heads I always learned something from what he had to say, as well as how to better formulate a case and defend a point. As the old Desmond Tutu saying goes, "Don't raise your voice, improve your argument."

Val Nasedkin has worked closely with Henk Kraaijenhof and has a wonderful grasp of how to develop energy systems. Not many coaches can talk intelligently about threshold motor units, functional biological systems, and amplitude frequency analysis, but Val can hold court on these and many more. He is also a pioneer in applying technology and data analysis thoughtfully and practically to test and enhance sports performance.

Another coach who showed me the necessity of looking far and wide for knowledge was Bill Sweetenham. Even though he only spoke to me and the other coaches at Wales for a little while initially, he went on to have a profound impact on my philosophy. He told me about Steven Pressfield's book *The War of Art* and on his recommendation, I went out and bought a copy. The next time Bill came to talk to the staff he saw the book on my desk, and I think this convinced him that I was serious about learning from him. After that, he added me to his email list and gave me advice anytime I needed it.

To help communicate better with his multi-national squad at Liverpool, Brendan Rodgers taught himself Spanish. I gave him a copy of Steve Peters's book *The Chimp Paradox* and he not only read it, but also brought Steve in to speak to the coaching staff.

I first met Eric Mangini when he was with the Cleveland Browns and was very impressed with him from the start. Our paths crossed again in San Francisco, where he was the assistant defensive coach and later became the defensive coordinator. He was very intelligent and cerebral. Like Tom Crean and some of the other fine coaches of his generation who didn't play the game at the highest level, Eric was constantly searching for ways to fill in his knowledge gaps. Sometimes those who've played the game are less eager to learn as they're not looking in from the outside.

In March 2017, Tom Crean left the Indiana Hoosiers men's basketball team after five years. Rather than spend his time licking his wounds or sitting at home feeling sorry for himself, Tom stayed busy. He got on the phone and began a year of traveling and learning from colleagues and competitors. Being a man who thrives on relationships and sharing knowledge, he used each day to improve his craft. Tom didn't limit himself to basketball. He visited NFL teams, college teams, and any environment he could learn from. Tom is a voracious reader, and this combined with all his trips fed an insatiable hunger to improve. He also acknowledged how humbling the experience was. But this is no surprise, as Tom is most helpful and genuine. Even when you're among the best, there are always opportunities to learn more.

Darren Lehmann was another lifelong learner. An incredible cricketer in his own right, Darren was the coach of Cricket Australia by the time I met him. What really impressed me most was his wonderful manner with coaches and other players. Darren was very conscious of and honest about what he didn't know and sought to fill his knowledge and skill gaps from experts in these areas.

Are you comfortable to the point of being complacent, or do you humbly recognize what you don't know?

COROLLARY

Real leaders are constantly looking to improve. They understand that there is always room to develop and grasp things they don't know. However, this never erodes their underlying confidence in what they do know. Maintain confidence, but stay hungry.

APPLICATION

Learn from everyone, including those outside your field. Ask many questions. Good leaders are aware of what they don't know and keep their fingers on the pulse of their industry. There are no issues, only opportunities. Time off from work should be viewed as a chance to learn, and a missed target used to eliminate future mistakes.

"We've all seen talented young players who get to a certain level but there comes a point where that talent will only take you so far. The great players go away and work on extra things. They work harder on their skills, they start having early nights and they think about their diet and training. That is what takes them to the next level."

— WARREN GATLAND

PLAY LIKE TARZAN, TRAIN LIKE JANE

47

Training must be hard and realistic to maximize the chance of winning.

When you play 14 years in the NFL, you either need to have a sense of humor from the get-go or must develop one. Justin Smith had one. "Cowboy" was among the funniest guys in the locker room, but on the field, he was all business. Justin had a rare ability to instantly switch on when it mattered most. He managed his reps carefully in practice, but the priority, as with Frank Gore and Patrick Willis, was on performing on game day. Nothing came above that.

I'd seen the same thing in Canterbury with Ashley Jones and the Crusaders players. All winners practice hard and prepare hard, but the best put the emphasis on the game. Ashley had a saying, "We don't want to train like Tarzan and play like Jane." Sure, weight room performance was important, but game performance was all that really mattered. On the other hand, the players that often don't make it do the opposite.

Amir Khan certainly trained and practiced the right way, and epitomized pure speed. I'd never seen anyone who was that quick on their feet, and his hands were just a blur when he was in the ring or pounding a heavy bag in the gym. Bernard Dunne was the same. You think you've seen speed until you train one of these guys. After he lost a world title fight, Bernard asked me to come train him. Though we were both living in Ireland at the time, his house was a couple of hours away from mine. I got up at 4 AM every morning, made breakfast, and was out the door by 5 AM so I could meet him at a gym near his house and have everything set up by 7 AM.

"THE ONLY PERFORMANCE THAT TRULY MATTERS IS GAME DAY PERFORMANCE."

Bernard was an incredibly hard worker and a brilliant boxer. I put together a comprehensive manual for him that covered everything from his gym regimen to nutrition and supplementation. Most athletes would've skimmed it at best. But like with Justin Smith, who was very deliberate in the supplements he took and where they came from, Bernard took his preparation so seriously that he not only read it word for word, but also took extensive notes. I was delighted for him that he won his return bout and then claimed the world title by beating Ricardo Cordoba on a memorable night in Dublin in front of a raucous home crowd. Even while Bernard was training hard at the pinnacle of boxing, he still prioritized his wife and kids and that really stuck with me.

Another fellow Irishman, Ronan O'Gara, was the all-time leading scorer in European rugby history at one time. He was very pleasant and polite, but had the focus of a sniper. I asked him once how often he practiced kicking, figuring that as he was late in his career he might be taking more time off. He looked at me as if I'd posed a very odd question and replied, "Every day." He has gone on to become an incredible coach at Canterbury and given his professionalism, I'm not surprised.

Great athletes practice hard. Very hard. But they always find a sense of humor or release. Some like Tommy Bowe, the Ulster and Irish rugby player, earn pilots' licenses while others learn musical instruments. The game can mean everything to them, but it's not the only thing in their lives. Does your team's internal attitude translate to game day performance, or are you just focused on winning practice?

COROLLARY

Often people confuse practice with performance. No doubt practice needs to be high quality. But never lose sight of the fact that the game is ultimately all that matters. No one wins on Sunday just because the preceding practices went well. Performance on whatever game day means for you and your organization has to be the priority.

APPLICATION

Always start from the game (in business, a product launch, a trade show, or all-company meeting; or in the military, an operation or major training exercise) and work backwards. The greatest praise should be reserved for actual performance, not the practice field. We avoid training like Tarzan and playing like Jane by ensuring practice is individualized to improve each team member's limiting factors, not merely reinforcing their strengths.

"Only those who never stand up, never fall down."

— JOHN KAVANAGH

HUMILITY
& PEOPLE

CONTROL THE CONTROLLABLES

48

Go through every scenario that might go wrong.

"Is there water on the bus?" Craig White asked.

The buses for the Welsh national rugby team were stationed outside the Vale of Glamorgan Hotel ready to depart. The team was seated downstairs in a semi-circle in silence, waiting for the head coach Warren Gatland to walk into the center to deliver his final words as he always did before a game. Tonight, we'd play the mighty All Blacks. I was likely bothering Craig (the performance director) about some insignificant coaching issue. He replied with a simple question that had an equally straightforward implication – control what you can control.

Sports science was starting to be seen as a panacea or cure for everything. This is not unique to sports. Around the same time, the business world and military also fell into the trap of tracking everything for its own sake. Some of us who were doing the monitoring mistakenly began thinking that we had a better guide to player performance than the coaches. There was a misconception that just because we could measure certain things, we fully grasped what was happening. This led many outside of the direct leadership circle to believe that they had a bigger influence on performance outcomes than they really did.

It's all too easy to become caught up in worrying about perceived problems without consulting our superiors. Often these aren't really factors that have a bearing on the overall mission, but because we can't see the whole picture and aren't in possession of all the facts, we start catastrophizing or focusing on the wrong priorities. I've occasionally been guilty of it. When things are uncertain, you need to ensure you're in control of your area of responsibility.

Another of the most valuable takeaways from my experiences within the military community is the need for attention to the details that concern you. It was here I started the habit of always carrying a small notepad in my hip pocket and having a pen with me wherever I went. When I forgot to bring the notepad, people would know, as I'd have reminders scribbled on the back of my hand. Working with operators taught me that you can't leave anything to chance when it comes to preparation.

"YOU CAN CONTROL MORE THAN YOU REALIZE."

It was from them that I also came to recognize the value of SOPs (standard operating procedures). To this day, I still use methods I learned and have built on for years. People can confuse the purpose of an SOP. It's true function is providing steps that work when you follow them in order, right up until when they don't and you have to improvise. This way, when you're under pressure, there's some element of order among the chaos so you can concentrate on winning.

The difference between winners and second place finishers is often that the latter lose focus on what they are actually in control of. By controlling everything you can actually influence, you reduce the number of things that you cannot and so leave less to chance. The key is knowing the difference and then managing those factors that you really can control.

A simple example is on-the-road and pre-game meals. Every time I traveled with a team and ate before games, my philosophy was to ensure everything was the same. I kept the details consistent at mealtime, from the number of people seated at each table to the food itself to cooking methods, and even condiments. I also tried to have us stay at the same hotels, so the staff would be familiar with how we did things.

As human beings, we have the capacity for change and choices – but when we have a greater or immediate priority such as a major competition – we prefer familiarity. So many minor decisions can sap our energy insidiously and though each one might be small, they can amount to a big stressor that's detrimental to performance. Save the major decisions for the major events.

Of even greater practical significance is the chance that something new or unusual would upset people before the game. From the moment that Phil Clarke, a former rugby league player, reminded me of an incident when several players got sick from eating seafood the night before a game, fish was off the menu from that moment forth. The comfort of having the same routine is also an advantage. The aim was always to limit the chaos to only what we couldn't control. The game and everything associated with it brings enough uncertainty, without having to add more through foolish or random food choices.

With players or anyone dealing with pressure situations, you want to preserve as much of what some refer to as their functional reserve (spare mental capacity) as possible. Players need to concentrate on what is important on game day and the buildup to it. If you can reduce the need to worry about unfamiliar meals, hotel rooms, and game plans you limit the stress of decision making. You should try to keep things predictable as the old adage, "There's comfort in routine," is very true. This is why I took it upon myself to think of every possible scenario and detail, so the players didn't have to drain their brainpower on unnecessary minutiae and could concentrate on what they did best. For tactical operators or elite athletes, the ability to manage change and proper decision making under pressure is important, but it is task specific and only necessary in certain scenarios.

When I worked with teams like the 49ers, Wales, and the University of Michigan, I created folders that contained a copy of every coach's and player's ID when we traveled for away games. This was very helpful anytime we needed identification at airports or in the case of an emergency. At hotels, the people behind the reception desk would get a list of staff names, their contact numbers, and their photos so that they would know who they were speaking with and could ensure no one could impersonate a team member. I always carried three copies of each.

Before we left for road trips, I produced a detailed document customized for every game. It was comprised of details on local hospitals, police stations, pharmacies, and so on. We listed travel times and routes from the hotel to the airport, stadium, and all the other places we were going to be visiting. In addition, we identified three routes for every location in case of emergency, road work, or some other unforeseen circumstance. Hotels were diagrammed, and meeting room sizes identified in case of issues with capacity or ceiling height for projectors. A year before our trip, a staff member would visit the hotel on a reconnaissance trip to photograph every possible meeting point and identify key features. We also assessed and took pictures of walk-through areas such as parking lots and green spaces, with special care given to noting the surfaces, where the sun would be shining in each half of the game, artificial lighting (if it was a night match), and, of course, possible viewing locations for prying eyes when players would be outdoors.

We came up with three options for just about everything and presented them to the head coach, who decided on the best one the week of the game. Then on the Wednesday beforehand, we gave the staff a packet that contained every conceivable travel detail.

On one reconnaissance trip for a rugby team, the guys got to the intended location to check out a training field, only to realize why they shouldn't have visited during winter. The practice field was under a few feet of snow, preventing them from assessing the playing surface.

Not all teams prepare to this level of detail, but it served two important functions for me and the teams I served. First, it gave us great comfort in controlling the controllables. Second, it gave us the ability to adapt to unforeseen events. Coaches like Eric Mangini, head coach of the Cleveland Browns, are very detail-oriented. Like

Eddie Jones and Sir Clive Woodward, he saw great value in thinking through every potential issue and having contingency plans in place.

Carlos Queiroz was also serious about nailing the particulars. I first met him and his assistant Mick McDermott in Dubai while Carlos was head coach of the Iranian soccer team. I'll never forget our conversation. It was on the side of a fabulous outdoor swimming pool at an exclusive hotel. Mick, Carlos, and I spent a couple of hours sketching out tactics and formations with complete indifference to the frivolity going on around us.

Both men were amazingly generous with their time and very patient with my questions. Carlos's attention to detail is legendary, down to the length of the grass. He wanted to know sideline dimensions and the angle the sun would be shining during different points of the game. Despite this, he also recognized the importance of a balance between players knowing what they needed to know in the moment and keeping the picture in mind.

Control what you can control. While you can't completely eliminate randomness or chance, you'll find you can anticipate and manage a lot more than you think.

Is your staff focusing on what matters, or have you allowed distractions to creep in?

COROLLARY

Over-preparation is rarely a bad thing – having the wrong people become distracted by it is. Delegate tasks to the appropriate team members and review their performance afterwards. Choose wisely.

APPLICATION

The preparation phase is key to having the confidence, calmness, and readiness necessary to deal with the chaos of elite performance. Routines and standard operating procedures can preserve emotional energy for the actual tasks that matter, not frivolous distractions.

"We spend the first two years of their life trying to get them to move and say 'Dada,' then spend the next 16 years telling them to sit down and shut up."

— KELVIN GILES

IT'S NEVER ABOUT THE TWO HOURS

49

The fight is won long before you take the field.

Gary Speed was one of English soccer's most respected players for decades. A key to his long and decorated soccer career was his dedication to taking care of himself outside of the team setting. He revealed to me that to play at the top level for many years, an athlete must look after themselves in the 22 hours or so a day that they're away from the squad. That's how Gary was able to set the record for the most Premier League appearances. He was serious about recovery and always showed up in shape and ready to go. Gary was also a true gentleman and a great role model for the younger players who looked up to him.

Justin Smith played for 13 years in the NFL. Guys like him don't turn up year in and year out ready to give their absolute best without dedication off the field. He would spend the offseason running hills and lifting weights first thing in the morning, and it showed every time preseason camp opened. Like Justin, Liverpool and England captain Steven Gerrard had achieved a lot in his career, but never rested on his laurels. He also took care of himself off the field and was determined to win at whatever cost. Stevie was very cautious and somewhat Irish, in the sense that he came off as dark and brooding at first. But once you got to know him, you discovered a wicked sense of humor.

Darren Burgess was head of fitness at Liverpool and Jordan Milsom, now Stevie's right-hand man at Glasgow Rangers was head of strength and conditioning. When I was getting to know them all, Jordan was often the brunt of good-humored banter and teasing from Stevie and Jamie Carragher. Stevie was loyal to a fault, as shown by the fact that, like Ryan Giggs, he spent his whole Premier League career with one team. Stevie set an example for every player in the England and Liverpool locker rooms that they needed to be similarly committed to showing up every Saturday prepared to excel.

Matt Nichol, who worked at the Toronto Maple Leafs, educated me in the importance of having a holistic perspective. Matt would travel anywhere to learn. He came to Wales to see the monitoring systems I developed and, more importantly, to see how Craig White and I were implementing them. Manchester United's Gary Walker and Richard Hawkins, two of the humblest soccer coaches in the Premier League, also made the journey to learn firsthand at a time when many coaches seemed to be getting too lazy to leave the comfort of their own offices.

"EVERYONE TRAINS FOR TWO HOURS.
THE OTHER 22 ARE WHAT MATTER."

Tony Strudwick has had a profound impact at Manchester United for over a decade. What I admire most about "Struds" is not just his craft, but also his honesty and pragmatism. Unless something works, he's not doing it. Along with Mark Howard, another incredibly smart soccer coach who I worked with at Blackburn Rovers in the Premier League, Struds recognized that health must be the basis for performance.

Finding balance in life can't be left to chance. I've made this mistake personally. You have to plan for it. To get as much done as I could each day, I used to have a white board at home in my kitchen. One line remained at the top of the board: 16:6:2. Visitors occasionally thought it was a Bible reference. But it was actually a reminder that I had 16 hours for work, six for sleep, and two for everything else. Sometimes the numbers might vary – e.g. 14:8:2, or in extreme situations, 18:4:2. It was a reminder to myself to work hard and be organized with how I allocated my time each day. This model is incredibly effective for getting work done, but it was too much for extended periods of time. Something has to break. You need to schedule rest – and lots of it after pushing hard. Otherwise you're going to fall apart sooner or later.

Craig White was a pioneer in this area. He was embracing practices that were outside the mainstream years before anyone else. Craig was constantly looking for new ways to enhance performance and recovery, even when these methods went against convention and popular "wisdom." Nobody in rugby (or any sport, for that matter) was doing yoga and meditation when he started introducing the players to it. He taught me the significance of treating the players as people first and athletes second, and to care about their overall wellbeing.

After one Crusaders game, Ashley Jones suggested meeting up for morning coffee the next day. I replied, "Sure, but don't you have to supervise the team's recovery session?"

"No, the guys do their own recovery," he replied.

Ash explained that the culture was strong enough to encourage them to do it without needing to be reminded by the coaching staff. Some would go to the beach, while others would do some light stuff on their own. Maybe a couple would go shopping with their wives or girlfriends. This was real recovery.

That's why *Game Changer* has health as the foundation for the four coactives of the TTPP model – Technical, Tactical, Physical, and Psychological. Unless you have a solid base, you cannot build up these other elements. This philosophy all originated from learning from the best in the world, from Christchurch to Toronto to Manchester, and many stops in between.

How much time do you give to observing the health and welfare of yourself and your team?

COROLLARY

People say elite sports are not healthy. There is truth to this. However, to have sustainable success you must have holistic psychological and physiological health. There are periods when you need to work hard, but everyone has a limit to the amount of pressure they can tolerate. You cannot neglect rest and recovery.

APPLICATION

Leaders who have the longest sustained careers typically maintain the best overall balance of life and work. Go all out for a little while now and again, but temper this with family life, friendships, and truly unplugged downtime.

"The purpose of the mission must be thoroughly understood beforehand, and the men must be inspired with a sense of personal dedication that knows no limitations. In an age of high technology and Jedi Knights we often overlook the need for personal involvement, but we do so at our own risk."

— ADMIRAL WILLIAM H. MCRAVEN

BE HONEST, NOT FAIR

50

Life isn't fair, and coaches can't be,
but you must be honest and candid.

Alastair Clarkson is the most successful Aussie rules coach of the modern era. Clarko created a dynasty at Hawthorn Hawks and is the longest serving coach in the Australian Football League (AFL). I first met him when I was working at Bolton and he was an assistant traveling with some other Aussie rules coaches. Clarko was quite reserved and intently watched what was going on around him. Our conversations after practice usually involved me doing most of the talking.

On the day before Clarko left, I asked him what changes he would make if he was in charge. Having not said much during his whole visit, the suggestions that followed were fascinating in both their scope and detail. Clarko outlined a list of things as long as his arm and had no qualms in telling me the brutal truth about what he thought we were doing wrong in everything from facility layout to player nutrition. He followed this up with advice on what to do better in each of these areas. Since then, we've met up and spoken many times. He's committed to relentless self-improvement and always blunt and direct. That cuts through a lot of nonsense and gets straight to the truth. Clarko has found the right balance of ruthlessness and caring for his players and coaches.

"BRUTAL HONESTY WILL ALWAYS BE RESPECTED."

My time with the 49ers also provided some useful lessons in candor, particularly from Harry "Doc" Edwards. He was a fascinating guy who passed on a lot of wisdom about coaching and particularly how to deal with problems effectively. Doc was a social activist for years and after seeing that Bill Walsh and his players had benefited from his perspective, Chip Kelly brought him in, first at the Eagles and then again when he came to the 49ers. Harry was not afraid to be argumentative and say exactly what was on his mind during meetings. His ability to challenge accepted norms brought value to a lot of the conversations we had.

The best coaches are direct and candid. Fairness is something different. Everyone cannot be treated the same. But fairness is understood by teams where there is complete openness. Nothing undermines team morale more than a dishonest head coach or leader. If there is no honesty, there is no trust, and without it, fairness becomes the issue that staff and players resort to complaining about.

I presented at a conference in Boston once and the world-renowned spine expert Stu McGill came up to me afterwards. My presentation dispelled many of the myths about sports science, including falsehoods about injury prediction and one-off testing being more important than continual monitoring. With someone who's such a pioneer, I was a bit worried about what he might say to critique my talk. But Stu humbled me by saying that not only did he agree with everything I'd said, but that it was also the best presentation he'd seen in 27 years because of my brutal honesty. You can't BS real experts in any industry with geek-speak, three-dollar words, or stats. Honesty, on the other hand, is always respected.

Are you consistent, do you have moral courage, and does your team know you are firm but honest?

COROLLARY

Rarely is there any reason not to be candid. While difficult conversations need to be had, these should be conducted in the context of trust and clarity. People will forgive unfairness when it's paired with openness, but not if there is dishonesty or obfuscation.

APPLICATION

Be open and transparent, but explain the situation and your rationale. Teams who have this level of honesty (and occasionally, conflict), build trust. With this, apparent unfairness is better understood. Being truthful also creates an atmosphere in which any disgruntled person is likely to come directly to you for answers, rather than complaining to their teammates.

"Rugby has always been a game for all shapes and sizes. You have the superstars and the fast guys who score the tries, but you also need the workhorses and the people who play all the other roles. Unless they all work together as a team, then it's really going to affect the performance. Everyone's got to rely on everyone else."

— WARREN GATLAND

GENERALISTS USE SPECIALISTS

51

In team sports you need generalists to integrate and apply, but also draw on specialists' experience.

My kitchen table was covered in paper, several laptops were open, and diagrams and charts littered the normally organized surface. A lesson was in full swing. I was the student and Kelvin Giles the professor. In any industry, we must learn from generations who come before us and there were few better teachers than Kelvin. The only qualities more remarkable than his generosity to young coaches were his experience and knowledge.

Kelvin was a former national and Olympic track and field coach and performance director. His breadth of experience was rare, as he was head coach at the Australian Institute of Sport, performance director of the famed Brisbane Broncos rugby league team, and also the UK's national track and field coach.

"Progress is made where paradigms meet," is one significant thing Kelvin taught me. What he was saying is that all too often, we like to stay within the comfort of our own specialized area – whether that's strength and conditioning, physical therapy, or whatever our field of expertise is. If we do so, most of the conversations we have are with other professionals in that little niche. There's nothing wrong with sharing ideas with our peers in this way, but we achieve the greatest advances when we cross-pollinate with experts in other disciplines.

When people have had different types of education, varied experiences, and unique perspectives, they come up with ways of doing things that you may never have even considered. It's also worth noting that no matter how versatile you are, you cannot be an expert in everything. So it's productive to create a wide network with contacts across multiple areas. That way, you can refer athletes to experts when you encounter specific issues that are outside your purview and also ask for their advice, while openly sharing what you're learning as well. Such a two-way exchange ensures you're not allowing your ideas to go stale and are constantly innovating.

"LEADERS CANNOT AFFORD TO SACRIFICE GENERALISM AT THE EXPENSE OF SPECIALIZATION."

While becoming an expert in a particular discipline is admirable, you also need to be well-versed in other complementary areas. One of these is psychology. Some teams seem to think that giving each player 20 minutes of weekly talk therapy is going to solve all their problems. In my experience, it usually fails to have much of an impact on players. You need to work on the culture first and once it's solid, only then consider working with a psychologist.

And if you do bring someone in, there needs to be a better, more intentional plan in place than just having them counsel players for a few minutes a week. Identify specific issues with certain players that can't be addressed by the coaches or your existing staff, and then look to a subject matter expert for targeted assistance.

Almost every pro and college squad has a full-time sports psychologist on staff, but it's not essential. This became clear when I was invited to present to the performance group at Manchester United's training facility. Once I'd been shown around and met most of the backroom team, Steve McNally asked me if there was anything they were missing. Manchester United brought in the vision coach Gail Stephenson long before any other Premier League team had even entertained such a notion.

They had an excellent fitness team, including Steve, Tony Strudwick, Richard Hawkins, Gary Walker, and Robin Thorpe. The only thing I could see that was missing was a team psychologist. When I put this to Steve, he abruptly stopped walking. We were passing through the coaches' corridor near the cafeteria. He pointed to the name plate on the door behind him. "As long as he's around, we'll never need a psychologist."

The plate read, "Alex Ferguson."

Point taken.

That isn't to say that there aren't talented people in that field, because there certainly are. But you can't just take a bolt-on approach to utilizing them or bring someone into a role to keep up with the Joneses.

Have you created a holistic team with integrated expertise, or do you have a siloed approach to problem solving?

COROLLARY

Specialists are necessary. Experts provide insight and are constantly investigating potential avenues to improve performance. Specialists are most effectively used in specific situations and it's often better to have them on call rather than on staff.

APPLICATION

In many cases, the use of expert knowledge fails for two reasons. Often there is a failure to understand the application and the needs of the organization properly. There can also be a theory gap – a failure to apply the expertise to make a difference. This is where generalists bridge the gap and help put the application in context.

"Everything I do is to make my mother and father proud."

— SHAUN EDWARDS

CIRCLE OF TRUST

52

Create a circle of trust and team spirit.

"If you have an embarrassing issue, we will tease you about things," Ronan O'Gara said. "It's because you're one of us and we care. In other teams they don't tease and that means they're talking behind your back. We're Munster. We don't do that here."

Nowhere is loyalty more apparent than among the Munster rugby team. It is one of the four major rugby clubs in Ireland. A team with a fiercely loyal following and long legacy of tough players. There, everything was on the table at all times and anything was open to question. In the best organizations, there is a brutal honesty that encourages continual dialogue. Players don't have agendas or egos. If we were going to do something differently, people wanted to know why. The coaching staff expected the squad to challenge their assumptions and methods, and they often improved on the original ideas.

Whether a player had been with the team for years or was in his first season, he was expected to speak up and share his opinion, even if it was unpopular. At Munster, winning wasn't just an occasional thing, it was the way they did things every day. Post-game reviews were candid, and no one was spared. Not even coaches. Everyone could be held to account by anyone – coaches and players alike. I called it a "naked review." No one was hiding anything, coaches had no seniority, and everyone in the room was on the same level.

As Ronan O'Gara explained, you could say anything to anyone's face and you could be equally assured that nothing would be said behind your back. Once I got over the initial shock of such ruthless honesty, I understood this team's strength of character. I found comfort in knowing that there was a circle of trust. Yes, there was constant teasing and joking and the expectation of absolute candor at all times, but I knew it was based on genuine love for teammates and fierce loyalty to Munster.

This circle of trust is vital to commitment. However, there is one caveat. You must have a moral and ethical code, even if it is unwritten. A circle of trust among a den of thieves breeds a code of conduct that leads to a toxic environment and the blind following of bad people. This was never in question at Munster, but it is common in some other organizations. Humility, honesty, and integrity must be at the core of any circle of trust.

The best leaders are typically the ones who emphasize the importance of these basic character traits. You have to be straight and direct with people, even when they're not going to like what you have to say. No one is perfect, but having truly exemplary human beings like Dougie Howlett,

Donncha O'Callaghan, Paul O'Connell, Ronan O'Gara, and many others assured that the circle of trust at Munster always had a strong moral compass.

This compass has to be calibrated by the leaders. If the head coach treats an assistant, player, or staff member dishonestly or talks badly behind their back, then others will see and hear about it and trust will begin to be questioned. As a teacher, you quickly notice a basic human desire. Children rarely care if you're "tough" or "easy" – but they do notice if you're not honest and fair to all. This is the same in sports, the military, and business.

That said, loyalty can bite you if you don't put the right people around you. If an assistant coach decides to be dishonest and not keep you informed or takes advantage of sponsor perks, you're going to have to deal with these issues quickly and decisively before they get out of hand to preserve the team's onus on trust and doing the right thing. But ultimately, that is your responsibility as a leader. The buck stops with you.

The leadership of senior players can go a long way to establishing a team culture founded on trust. Kevin Nolan was a great leader in the Bolton Wanderers locker room. Sam Allardyce often jokingly called him "the trade unionist" because Kevin was a vocal advocate for the squad and was never afraid to speak up when he felt there was an issue or disagreed with something Sam or any of the other coaches had said. When a team has a culture founded on trust and openness, debate is actually promoted and helps produce better outcomes. This was one of Sam's greatest strengths in my opinion. Even when Kevin and Sam had different viewpoints, it never descended into a serious shouting match. They'd go back and forth a little and eventually find a reasonable middle ground. Sam was smart and he encouraged Kevin to speak up. This meant whispering and grumbling were rare.

Every great team I've been around has a similarly open dialog. This includes the Special Operations community. One of these elite groups prides themselves on having a "rankless and classless" approach to self-management. If you have something to say, you're expected to say it. After-the-fact revelations or opinions cost lives. Sometimes these guys need to have the level of vulnerability and awareness to raise their hand and say, "I'm not ready for this mission." It's better for them to stay behind than to go and put themselves and everyone else at risk. Such honesty is a critical component of trust in such situations.

"CANDOR CONVEYED IN A CIRCLE OF TRUST INSPIRES GREAT ACHIEVEMENTS."

The coaching staff also has a great responsibility in this domain. Jack Harbaugh often told me how valuable conflict was in successful teams. He was of the opinion that trust was the first characteristic you had to develop to have a sustainably excellent organization. I would argue that honesty is critical to develop that trust. Conflict is useful and can even be beneficial, but only if there's a bedrock of honesty. Jack was right in saying that you can get quicker answers through constructive disagreements and that if you have sufficient trust, everyone would get on board when you came up with a resolution to an issue.

Loyalty isn't only essential among the players, but also the coaching staff. A primary reason for Alastair Clarkson's unparalleled success in Aussie rules football is his ability to suppress his ego. Instead of just trying to further his own interests, he has always focused on doing everything he can to further his fellow coaches' professional development. This has led to a fierce sense of loyalty within Hawthorn's small, tight-knit unit, which includes the outstanding David Rath and head of fitness David Russell. They've both refused many job offers from elsewhere because they know they have something special where they are. The sum total at Hawthorn is better than anything they'd find at another team.

When I first encountered Bryce Cavanagh, he was the performance coach for West Indies cricket and I was at the Welsh national rugby team. Bryce soon joined Munster rugby, where we worked together. The coach at the time, Tony McGahan, was followed by Rob Penney and Axel Foley, but Munster retained its own unique culture. Axel was a Munster and Irish legend and had achieved a lot in his playing days and that carried significant weight in the locker room.

Bryce and I were both early risers and we'd get up at 5:30 or 6 AM to go grab coffee in Cork City on the way to practice. Then in the evening, Bryce and I would stay up late talking about performance. They were long days, but it never seemed like work to me because I enjoyed being around the team so much.

Are your people loyal and, more importantly, do they know *you* are loyal and supportive of them?

COROLLARY

Loyalty is critical to any success, but it must be reciprocated and based on a strong ethical and moral code first and foremost. Blind loyalty only leads to blind followers and this culminates in rules being broken when pressure is at its highest.

APPLICATION

Leaders show unfailing loyalty to their team. They support them when times are at their most difficult, not just in their professional life, but also (and perhaps more importantly) in their personal life as well. A true leader understands that when the time comes for their staff to support them and the company, such unwavering loyalty will be returned.

"There are scientists who will tell you that spirit, because it can't be measured, doesn't exist. Bollocks. It does exist."

— SAM ALLARDYCE

ONE MAN'S MEAT
IS ANOTHER MAN'S POISON

53

There's no real work-life balance or division between performance and recovery – they roll into one.

Charlie Francis was adamant that recovery was just as important as training, and that the two were indivisible. Yes, what his athletes did on the track and in the weight room mattered, but it was how they recovered that ultimately determined their adaptation and progress. Charlie went beyond the reductionism that had started to take hold in sports and viewed the athlete as a whole person – mind, body, and spirit intertwined as a whole. Believe it or not, recovery has not always been held in such high esteem as it is now.

When I started work in the NFL, Jim Harbaugh called me into his office overlooking the San Francisco 49ers training facility. When I came in, I saw he was poring over the team schedule. He leaned across the desk and handed me the week's training and practice schedule. "Fergus, what do make of this?" he asked, "And when do you think the day off should fall?" The NFL mandates that players have one day a week off. I told him that ideally it should be the day after the game.

This is because it gives the players the chance to spend time with friends and family, provides coaches the opportunity to review film in detail, and gives a particular rhythm to each week. Giving the coaches time to assess what went right and wrong during the game is incredibly valuable. Leaving players to their own devices on the day after the game would provide Jim and his staff a 24-hour buffer zone between whatever emotions the team felt right after the final whistle and how the coaching staff would frame the game's events in the first practice or film session of the new week. However, this went against almost every scientific and popular approach that suggested recovery workouts should be the day after a game.

The only proviso was the age and experience of the team. With younger teams, you need good habits and giving the day off after a game might not be suitable. But with older and more experienced teams where professionalism is a trademark (like the 49ers that year), they will always do their due diligence with recovery and many will come in to the facility for treatment post-game on their own initiative.

"NOT EVERYONE REACTS THE SAME WAY TO SIMILAR EVENTS."

When it comes to balancing the recovery aspect of performance, managing training loads is essential. Working with professional athletes, you realize they need both stimuli recovery for adaptation. For a while, many experts were suggesting that creatine kinase and inflammation markers couldn't be elevated beyond a certain point or they'd become extremely detrimental. But the stimulus had to be great enough to prompt growth and repair. If you went too far in utilizing recovery methods that blunted the stimulus, then you wouldn't get the kind of adaptation the training was designed to produce.

Through a combination of diligent research and years of practical acumen, many coaches I'd worked with had fine-tuned their programming to introduce just enough stress without overloading players. You push them hard, but also make sure they are being taken care of.

Some people took this too far. In some sports, recovery was viewed as something that had to be avoided or manipulated to enable higher and higher training mileage. Steve Dank became embroiled in the Essendon and Cronulla doping scandals. Through work with the Manly Sea Eagles, Gold Coast Suns, and other teams, he used methods such as supplementing with Lactaway or Actovegin to support the aerobic system in recovery. Victor Conte had a similar path with supplementation approaches through his company BALCO. But these methods crossed ethical guidelines in many sports and began to blur the lines between legal and illegal performance enhancement, if not cross them completely. The danger with supplements of any kind – both on the banned substances list and those that governing committees deem acceptable – is that they can blunt adaptation.

Recovery shouldn't just be an add-on or afterthought. It can be comprised of many factors and means different things to different people. One study I did with two players early in my career demonstrated this clearly. I observed them in detail for a 24-hour period after a very hard training block. One was single and headed home to relax on his couch for the evening after training. His plan was to watch TV, eat, and get to bed early to rest. The other was married with three kids and was transitioning from training to the chaos of his daughter's birthday party.

We both know which environment I expected to be most supportive to the recovery process. However, what was surprising was that the older player seemed to recover fastest based on all the metrics. Why was this? He explained that while he found the birthday party noisy and frantic, afterwards the family went for a quiet stroll together and he went to bed reasonably early. The younger player chatted with some friends on the phone, didn't meet anyone, watched TV, and played video games late into the night. So his recovery ended up being worse, even though he had fewer obligations. Of course, there are multiple other factors to be considered, but the underlying point was that what's relaxing to some players is not to others.

Pádraig Harrington told me how playing poker the night before a tournament was something he could never do, but for some golfers this was the best way to wind down. In contrast, Pádraig liked to be alone, relax, and prepare on his own.

Everyone needs time to recover. But one man's meat is another man's poison. What is recovery to one is detrimental to another. The dosage is also critical. For some, playing cards or watching TV late into the night works, but for most, a few hands or a short episode of their favorite sitcom is plenty. I learned to educate and always provide my athletes with options rather than making something I thought might enhance recovery become a stressor.

Is everyone treated as an individual and allowed to find their own way to achieve balance?

COROLLARY

Recovery is necessary, but you must be careful enforcing it as a rule or it can become another stressor. Educate people in how they can recover and rest and give them options. Even what can be deemed social events that are planned as relaxation can become detrimental to people if they are fatigued and would benefit more from time off.

APPLICATION

In today's world in which work has a more international and tech-obsessed component to it than ever before, work and rest roll into one. More flexible management is needed to allow workers some volition in their chosen time off and recovery. If you expect your people to be available to answer emails or calls after hours, then you need to give them a little grace during the day. It shouldn't be work-life balance, but rather the reverse, in which rest and work are intertwined and reasonably calibrated.

"It is the players who make the system, not the other way round."

— CARLOS QUEIROZ

WE WON'T REALLY KNOW
FOR 20 YEARS

54

**Understand the need to look after yourself
before you can help others.**

I first met Biff Poggi at the University of Michigan when he
strolled into my office. Biff, who was the associate head
coach, came in and sat in the big soft lounge chair I had
placed in front of my desk. I had no idea who this gregari-
ous man with a huge smile, booming laugh, and an apparent objection to wearing socks was. At first, I didn't know if
Biff was absentminded, too lazy to wear socks, or making
a fashion statement that I was out of touch with, which is
quite conceivable.

Biff's role was to assist the staff, come up with procedures for the program, and support the head coach Jim
Harbaugh. The great irony was that these two men were
polar opposites in terms of personality. Biff is engaging,
genuinely caring, and an excellent people manager. He has

the rare combination of being incredibly creative and still getting things done – but most of all, he can win football games. In your life you will meet thousands of people. If you're truly lucky, one of them will be Biff Poggi.

Biff coached at Gilman High School in Baltimore, where he had been a student himself along with his friend Joe Ehrman many years before. Their story was encapsulated in Jeffrey Marx's best-selling book *Season of Life*. After Gilman objected to Biff paying for scholarships for disadvantaged kids, he moved on to coach at St. Frances Academy in inner city Baltimore. The school is in the infamous area where the hit TV series *The Wire* was filmed. Kids go to school each morning in the depressing shadow of Baltimore Prison, walking past boarded-up houses, and stepping over drug paraphernalia.

But spend a few minutes with these kids, Biff, and his coaching staff, and you'll immediately notice the joy and love he brings to their lives (you can see it for yourself in the ESPN documentary *Battle of Baltimore*). As a reminder of how fortunate I am, I often send a portion of my speaking fees to St. Frances.

In Biff's football program, twelve kids are legally homeless and up to nine have lost a family member to gun violence. The coaches help these young men overcome their tough circumstances by providing them with structure, compassion, and, above all, unconditional love. Biff also teaches invaluable lessons about how to conduct themselves, be professional, and buy into a team concept that transcends sports.

"PERSON FIRST. ATHLETE SECOND."

At other schools or universities that have a lack of accountability, athletic directors are often too lazy and self-centered to worry about anything else other than their golf handicap. In an era when the most disadvantaged of kids in our country are offered scholarships to play sports and need the most care, many just ignore this and exploit their position of influence. The role of sports should be to teach young people skills that prepare them for life.

Biff's approach has always been person-first, athlete second. His philosophy toward these troubled teens can be encapsulated in a single question: "What can I do for you?" A lot of them beat the odds to earn college scholarships. Biff's example showed me how profoundly a caring coach who is genuinely invested, fiercely protective, and completely committed can change people's lives.

Like Biff, Wayne Bennett has a special ability to nurture the most troubled players and, in many cases, help them play the best rugby of their career. Wayne knows that many squad members have already proven their skillset on the field. He understands that developing them as people can restore their love of the game and unlock their true ability and potential, even after other coaches have written them off. Wayne genuinely cares for every one of his athletes and staff members, and they reward him by giving their all every weekend.

The greatest ability of a coach is to get someone to want to play for them. This is why people like Biff and Wayne are very, very rare. Quite a lot of players who came to Wayne's teams late in their careers had been labeled troublemakers or underachievers. His nurturing style empowered them to finally live up to their potential. He believed that what's happening in a player's life has more impact on their play than anything they can do in the weight room or on the practice field.

Love is also a powerful and binding force between coaches. When Jack Harbaugh lost his job at Kentucky, the first person to call him was his old boss, Bo Schembechler, who wanted to make sure that he had a new position lined up. Bo also showed Jack a good example in another way: he truly loved his coaches. Often when staff salaries were finalized, those with no kids noticed they were making a little less than coaches with families, even if their experience was comparable. Any extra money went to a coach and usually the one with the most mouths to feed. Why? Bo cared. When the head coach is genuinely invested in his or her staff, they demonstrate their commitment to their spouses and kids as well.

Many coaches tend to focus on the players exclusively or think about what the fans want, when in reality they should concentrate on meeting the needs of their direct subordinates, who will in turn take care of the players. I'll leave you with an extract from *Season of Life* that sums up all you need to know about Biff Poggi and the true meaning of coaching:

"At a cookout after the scrimmage – family members included – this woman casually asked Biff how things were looking for the team. How successful did he think the boys were going to be?

'I have no idea,' Biff said. 'Won't really know for twenty years.'"

Are you too worried about your customers at the expense of your staff?

COROLLARY

You must have a vison for how the team will perform. You need to create an ideal, a goal. Just worrying about the players without direction is not going to lead to success. Have a vision, but look after your people first.

APPLICATION

We often only worry about performance, but we have far less control over game day results than we'd like to believe. We can impact the input more than the output. Take care of the person and the outcome will take care of itself.

"I'd rather lose a game than lose a kid"

— BIFF POGGI

DISCIPLES DIFFER.
LEADERS AGREE.

55

Go to the source, not the disciples.

In a nondescript industrial park lies an unremarkable warehouse outside Columbus, Ohio. There is no sign, no name, nothing to signal what lies behind it. Morning after morning for decades, the strongest men in the world have walked through the doors to train at an elite, invitation-only facility. In a small torture chamber, they lift bars and weights that look nothing like the polished colored plates or machines you find in modern college or professional NFL team weight rooms. Under a true pioneer in the world of strength, they train to move rusted battered weights, setting world records by a half inch. 25lbs is always 25lbs – polishing it doesn't make it lighter.

Louie Simmons owns and runs this gym. He has trained and prepared more record holders in powerlifting than anyone in the world. Louie developed his Westside Barbell method over many years of study, theory, and practice. An accomplished athlete in his own right, he's one of only five lifters to record elite totals in five different weight classes.

He has written many books and openly shares his concepts, which many have copied. But there is only one Louie and only one Westside. Having studied the Westside Method for years and trained many athletes in the methodology, I thought I knew a lot about it. But when Louie invited me to come visit I also believed that many of his approaches would be in direct conflict with what I had learned from other coaches in different sports because powerlifting is so different than team settings. But sitting across from Louie in his office, discussing many of his principles with him, Tom Barry, and John Quint, I found more similarities than differences.

This is not the first time I've had such a realization, but it underlined again for me the need to go directly to the source, to tap leaders and ignore advocates or second-hand disciples. When you discuss techniques with Louie, you find that he is not only a gold mine of information and experience, but also a sophisticated thinker. Delve deeper into Louie's mind and principles and you find out how solid his logic and understanding really are.

"DON'T WASTE TIME ON SECONDHAND INFORMATION. GO TO THE SOURCE."

Sitting with Louie was somewhat of a déjà vu experience. For years before I went to stay with Charlie Francis in Canada, I had read and re-read his coaching book *Training for Speed* and his fascinating autobiography *Speed Trap* many times. I'd also spent hours poring over his website forum, where people would debate aspects of his Vertical Integration system that encourages coaches to train each one of their athletes' attributes to some degree at all times. As a result of all this reading and research, I had a pretty firm idea about what Charlie's methods were. These informed the 20 questions I'd written down to ask him.

A few weeks later on the flight home, I pulled out the piece of paper to see if I had missed anything. Going slowly down the list of questions, I realized I hadn't gotten an answer to a single one. It slowly dawned on me that the reason was simple: I wasn't even asking the right questions.

This taught me a valuable lesson about the dangers of misinterpreting the written word or worse still, second-hand information. Yes, you can glean insights from what an expert writes or says in an interview, but you won't get the full story unless you actually spend time with them and leave your preconceptions at the door.

Charlie wouldn't allow me to remain stuck in lazy thinking or my off-the-mark deductions. He frequently answered a question with a question, forcing me to clarify and simplify my thinking as he had done over several decades to continually refine his coaching philosophy. He had a wonderful ability to look at problems in an unexpected way and by using a different lens to the one most coaches would, he'd usually devise a unique solution. I learned from him that to come to solid conclusions, you have to ask the right questions.

Chris Cooper played in the NFL for the Raiders and 49ers for almost 10 years. He was another rare student of the game who, like Pádraig Harrington, could explain the unique demands athletes deal with as both players and people. When Chris retired from pro football, he set up a facility in Dublin, California near the Raiders facility where he played for years to help the next generation of players. Chris used his firsthand NFL experience to provide targeted training, but, more importantly, offered tailored recovery modalities that he had battle-tested at the highest level.

He brought world-renowned Don Chu, one of the first trainers to introduce plyometrics to the West, to his facility. I had plenty of questions about plyometrics, as there were many misconceptions, but when I spent time with Don, I saw that his principles were in line with experts like Dan Pfaff, Stu McMillan, and Louie Simmons.

Just as I had some false assumptions about Don's work, so too did I fundamentally misunderstand the tactical periodization approach of Vitor Frade until I went to Portugal to learn from him directly. I was introduced to him by José Tavares and as I don't speak Portuguese and Vitor speaks very little English, José generously acted as our translator. As with Charlie Francis and Louie Simmons, I had just about everything about Vitor and his methods wrong. When I gave him examples of European teams I thought were using tactical periodization well, he chuckled, as their methods weren't at all in line with his philosophy. My time with Vitor convinced me again that to truly understand someone's thinking, you need to go directly to the source whenever it's possible. You can't get the same level of comprehension from other people's hand-me-down interpretations of their methodology.

I had the very same experience with the renowned author Simon Kuper, who has written for decades on the use of analytics in soccer and other team sports. He co-authored the best-selling *Soccernomics: Why England Loses,*

Why Spain, Germany, and Brazil Win, and Why the US, Japan, Australia—and Even Iraq—are Destined to Become the Kings of the World's Most Popular Sport with Stefan Szymanski. They interviewed me because they agreed that going to the source is always the most effective way to find the meaning and understand the context of someone's teaching and ideas.

The same lesson repeated itself with someone who wasn't directly involved in sports. Carol Dweck is a professor at Stanford who wrote the book *Mindset: The New Psychology of Success*. I met her when I was working at the 49ers and over dinner with her and her husband, I discussed the application of her ideas to my situation in particular. Carol was very gracious to give me some fascinating insights. A big takeaway was that after reading her book, I thought I knew exactly what a growth mindset was. But in sitting down with Carol, I saw that I only had a surface-level understanding. That evening she was able to share the subtleties of her approach and provide practical advice for creating a growth mindset at any organization without forcing it.

Carol was also interested in my perspective on that side of things, which gave me some validation. That's another benefit of going directly to the source. Sometimes people don't want to spend the time or money to do that, but then they miss out on the true value you get from picking great minds. It's only in meeting them face to face that you can get a detailed interpretation of their ideas and learn how you might apply these to your profession. And though some experts are too busy to return your calls or meet with you, many others are far more welcoming than you might expect.

Are you making decisions based on firsthand knowledge or secondhand rumors?

COROLLARY

It's not always easy and grasping complex principles can be difficult. It takes time to study and understand how things work, but it requires insight and experience to find the right principles and then align them with your beliefs.

APPLICATION

Gleaning from books or papers is one thing, but nothing beats going directly to the source. Don't focus excessively on the methods without due recognition of what's under-pinning them.

"Believe it or not, we actually practice putting the ball down properly. It is a bugbear of mine."

— SHAUN EDWARDS

NEVER AVOID AN OPPORTUNITY TO SHUT UP

56

Allow people to learn and don't always feel the need to talk.

The Welsh rugby players collapsed on the grass. Craig White, the head of performance, had just blown the whistle after a brutal training session. Drenched in sweat, some of the guys were shirtless and most socks were down around their ankles. I stood beside "Whitey" near the sideline. Bodies were strewn everywhere, having dropped where they stood when the whistle blew to signal the end of practice. I stepped forward with water and began to help the guys up off the ground. Whitey grabbed the back of my shirt. I looked at him and he nodded his head to follow him. We walked off the side of the field in silence.

When we were out of the players' earshot he said, "Let them be. Sometimes you have to let them pick up the pieces." It wasn't being cruel or uncaring. Whitey was smart. He knew that on certain occasions, you don't need to say anything to the players because they'll absorb the lesson themselves just by going through an experience.

Brendan Rodgers was a master communicator, as well. I can honestly say that I never heard him criticize a player. He was always encouraging the squad. Everything was positive, supportive, and instructional. He never raised his voice, or criticized a coach in front of a player. He didn't give long team talks. Acutely aware of his players' attention and their optimism, Brendan was a diligent student of the game and allowed players to learn for themselves when interrupting would have been easier at times.

"YOU DON'T ALWAYS HAVE TO SPEAK."

He's not the only soccer genius who was a master of player management. Toon Gerbrands was the football director at AZ Alkmaar, a soccer team who play in the Dutch league and the only squad outside the top three teams in Holland to win the national title in the past 20 years. Toon told me two very important things I've always practiced to this day, both of which he learned from Louis van Gaal. Louis would never correct a player on tactical issues in private. He always did it in front of the whole team for two reasons. Firstly, by speaking to the player in front of their teammates, he communicated something once that he'd otherwise have to tell all 22 squad members individually. Saying it just once ensured clarity of message. Secondly, it meant that no player could leave his office after a private meeting and claim Louis had said something that he didn't. Anything personal, however, Louis addressed in private.

Warren Gatland also said very little in practice. In training camps, he'd get the players to increase their effort level just by walking through the gym. He rarely raised his voice, smiled at the guys, and broke tension with humor. Early in the week he observed and encouraged, but only loudly enough so nearby players could hear him. However, on game day he spoke with authority and gave crystal clear instructions to the team. To a man, the squad listened intently.

Warren once gave a certain player a great piece of advice: "Never refuse the offer to speak if you're asked your opinion." He meant that when you're asked to voice your views by a coach you have everyone's attention and should make the most of the opportunity. This doesn't happen often, but many players either refuse or are caught off guard when asked. Always be prepared and pay attention.

Coaches who talk too much and unnecessarily can make players numb to their voice. They often lose impact on game day, when it's needed most. These are the same coaches who tend to micromanage and fail to transfer ownership to their assistants and players. Words are powerful, but silence can be equally potent when used properly.

What kind of leader are you? Do you always have to be heard, or do you use silence just as effectively?

COROLLARY

Words can be used to gain trust, inspire, and direct people. But actions must follow to demonstrate authenticity. Words alone are never enough.

APPLICATION

Don't overuse your voice unless it's absolutely necessary. Never talk just to talk. Speak to encourage. If something needs to be said as constructive criticism, say it in private. Carefully decide between things that should be said in public and conversations that need to take place behind closed doors.

"I would prefer to tell a young player what to do than how to do it."

— GREG CHAPPELL

GREG CHAPPELL ST.

57

Be humble. Humility is based on your internal self-image, whereas pride comes from what others think about you. Understand the difference.

I crumpled my tired body into the car. Pat Howard had been the head coach at Leicester Tigers years before and now had moved on to reinvigorate Cricket Australia's fortunes. He'd brought me in to consult with the organization for a few weeks. Of all the general managers I've been around, Pat was one of the most impressive. At times I'd forget how young he was, considering he's played on two continents, earned twenty caps for Australia, coached the Tigers, and went on to manage one of Australia's most storied national organizations.

Throughout the week, I'd presented on two main topics: "Thinking Differently – Successful Innovation in Sports" and "High Performance Habits – Lessons from Other Sports." The most enjoyable part of my experience was the engagement and interaction with the experienced coaches. Rod

Marsh and Greg Chappell were two of the most famous and legendary figures in cricket. They were also the two who were most involved in the team's activities and discussions. To have played and coached as much as they had, I'd have forgiven them if they hadn't wanted to listen to me coming in with all these new-fangled ideas, but it was actually the complete opposite.

Back in the car, Darren Holder was driving me to the airport. Greg, in a genuinely touching act, had given me a book, *First Tests: Great Australian Cricketers and the Backyards That Made Them* by Steve Cannane, as a gift before I left. I was impressed and appreciative. As we pulled out of the Cricket Australia parking lot, I asked Darren for his address so I could return the favor when I got back to the States. He leaned over and pointed up at the road sign. It read, "Greg Chappell St." The whole two weeks, a man who hadn't needed to learn any more about the game took part in the conversations with me though it was his first professional opportunity. I'd witnessed true humility from a legend whose name was on the street where he went to work each day.

"HUMILITY IS AT THE CORE OF ALL GREAT LEADERS."

One day at the San Francisco 49ers, we had a girl's youth soccer team visit in the offseason to see the new Levi's Stadium and its recovery facilities. I hung back as the team walked through and was joined at the back of the room by a long blonde-haired lady who obviously was a coach. We chatted for a bit and discussed the differences between European and American approaches to the "beautiful game."

After she left, a Niners assistant coach approached me and asked, "Have you worked with Brandi before?"

"No. Who's Brandi?" I replied

"You were talking to Brandi Chastain, the US women's soccer player who scored the winning penalty in the 1999 World Cup final. I thought maybe you'd coached her before." Just as with Greg, she'd been too humble to point out who she was or make a big deal of it. Instead, Brandi was interested in my perspective.

Humility is not something that is unique to older players or veteran coaches. During my time visiting Ashley Jones at Canterbury Crusaders, I'd get to the weight room by 6:30 AM each morning to make the most of every day, spend time with Ashley, and be around the players and staff as much as possible. Many mornings, one player would get there around the same time and let me into the simple, workmanlike gym under the Crusaders stand. "Yoda," as the players called him, was rehabbing an Achilles injury (at about 115 kilograms or 250 pounds, he was obviously a prop and so bore zero resemblance to the real, diminutive Jedi Master). His diligence was impressive. Every morning he was there first to work on his rehab exercises. I would strike up a casual conversation, but despite my eagerness to learn from him, he ended up asking most of the questions. He told me that he'd been to Ireland and England, asked exactly where I was from, and we chatted about hobbies and the rehab process.

Being in the Crusaders gym back then was like walking into a melting pot of the world's richest rugby talent. Even in those days, they were the most dominant club team in the world. Led by Richie McCaw, the Crusaders also had Aaron Mauger, Kieran Read, Brad Thorn, Campbell Johnstone, Chris Jack, Leon MacDonald, Corey Flynn, Wyatt Crockett, Casey Laulala, and, of course, Dan Carter.

Almost everyone in sports has heard the term "sweeping out the sheds" about the All Blacks. But few realize that years before it became a foundational habit of the national team, it was practiced at Canterbury. Players carried out the cones to help Ashley and Luke Thornley set up the field before practice and cleared it up again afterwards. Nobody made post-workout shakes for you here – you made your own.

One other aspect of the Crusaders' culture was humor. Chris Jack was wisecracking and cutting any player who got too confident down to size. Campbell Johnstone, Corey Flynn, and Wyatt Crockett were continuously firing verbal barbs at each other like feuding brothers. And even the golden boy of world rugby, Dan Carter, had his own sense of dark, self-depreciating humor. This symphony of hard work, focus, and kidding around was masterfully orchestrated by Ashley, Luke, and Robbie Deans.

The humility of the group was typified by Aaron Mauger, who had captained both the All Blacks and Crusaders. He was interested to find out more about Leicester Tigers, who he'd agreed to move to after the end of the current Super Rugby season was over.

That evening back at my hotel I wondered how many times Aaron had played for the All Blacks. I flipped open my laptop, went to the All Blacks website, and looked through the pictures of current squad members. As I scrolled down, I noticed a familiar face: Yoda. Rather than being Luke Skywalker's green mentor, he was actually Greg Somerville, a mainstay for the Crusaders for years and at one point, the longest serving prop in All Blacks history with 66 caps. Yet from our first talk onward, Greg had never even mentioned he played for the All Blacks, said who he was, or tried to impress me by regaling all that he had achieved. Instead, he was only interested in getting to know me and, when we were done talking, focused on rehabbing his ankle so he could get back on the field with his teammates. His willingness to learn, curiosity about others, and complete lack of ego left a lasting impression on me.

Neil Jenkins was another player whose biggest asset (outside of his technical ability) was his steadfast humility. He was one of the best fly-halves in world rugby but never once bragged about his prowess. Even when I asked Neil about his career, he kept trying to pivot the conversation by asking questions about me because he didn't like talking about himself. Neil was also dedicated to preparing the next generation of players for greatness. He'd go out of his way to help someone improve. I saw a similar humble attitude years later in Colin Kaepernick. He'd always stay late signing photos, caps, and jerseys for fans, even as his teammates drifted away.

Eric Cressey has a gym in Boston and is a top trainer in baseball. I met him almost 20 years ago when he came to Ireland. He was a young, down-to-earth guy and the only American I'd ever seen with paler skin than me (the old adage about an Irishman only having two tones – pasty or burned – is a stereotype, but an accurate one!). At the time, Eric was just getting his first facility going and had recently completed his second book. The thing that made the biggest impression on me was how humble he was, despite being a rising star in his profession. He had done a huge amount of research on the function and mobility of the shoulders and ankles, and had a solid foundation of knowledge that he was able to present in an engaging way. But though he was well on the way to the top of the sports performance ladder, Eric never bragged about his achievements or thought highly of himself. Instead, he was eager to learn, discover new things, and broaden his knowledge.

When I was in the early days of my role with the Welsh national rugby team, Marco Cardinale was very helpful. Like Sir Clive Woodward, he made time for someone he'd never met before. Marco was probably the only sports scientist I'd met whose early experience was coaching handball in Italy. When we were introduced, he was working with the British Olympic Association under Sir Clive Woodward. Marco wrote a great book on strength and conditioning (along with Robert Newton and Kazunori Nosaka), *Strength and Conditioning: Biological Principles and Practical Applications.*

Henk Kraaijenhof once showed me a photo of him, Marco, Carmelo Bosco, and a couple of others. It was this incredible combination of old masters and young, up-and-coming apprentices. The lesson was that if you're more experienced, you have to be willing to share what you've learned with the next generation. And if you're just starting out, you should challenge yourself by being around the leaders in your field and being open to their tutelage.

Is your team displaying the correct balance of humility and confidence, or has arrogance taken hold?

COROLLARY

Unshakeable confidence comes from an understanding of your abilities as well as recognition or acceptance of your limitations. Preparation and performance under pressure breed confidence. When it leads to arrogance and complacency, it becomes lethal.

APPLICATION

The only way to avoid complacency is to maintain humility and honesty at all times. You must be vulnerable enough to realize that you're not perfect and, like everyone else, have limiting factors to improve. Without humility, we are blind to areas we can develop and will never reach our full potential.

"Football is not a linear process. It is not a sum of things: If you do this, plus that, you will achieve this. The coach must consider every aspect, of the individual, of the team. Football is not two-dimensional. It is multidimensional."

— VITOR FRADE

YOUR 2ND STRING IS MORE IMPORTANT THAN YOUR 1ST

58

Why backups are more critical and
harder to identify than your starters.

People often think that the only time your backups really
matter is when injuries occur. This is a very myopic perspective. There are many reasons why your second string
is arguably more important than your first. Munster,
Canterbury, Wales, and Liverpool all have very conscious
approaches to player growth. In Europe, rugby and soccer teams generally have very structured ways to develop
talent through academy systems. This means that the gap
between the starters and their backups is as small as possible and players are prepared and ready if called upon to
replace an injured teammate. US sports (the NFL, NBA,
and even at the college level) tend to look for instant solutions with less focus on the longer-term development of
the player, let alone the welfare of the person. And as they

don't have youth academies, they can't bring younger play-ers up to the first team squad when the time is right (or ingrain the club's system of play and standards for many years before they make their senior debut).

The single biggest reason for a structured develop-ment approach is to improve the standard of play. Your first string must be able to compete at a very high level in prac-tice. As a coach, you can manage the loading and stress using small-sided game or drill design, field or pitch size, and work/rest times. In team sports, game intelligence and ability are greater compensators than physical quali-ties. The best way to cultivate these is competition. Playing against good quality athletes at the highest level possi-ble – in practice – is also essential. The decision-making and movement demands, reactions, and forces required in such a setting are as close to replicating game day condi-tions that you can get.

This realistic preparation decreases the probability of a drop off in standards if a replacement is made by choice or forced when a first-string player is injured. His or her teammates have seen the substitute in action under pres-sure up close and know they can deliver. This maintains confidence and the belief in a positive outcome. These are critical factors in any elite group's performance.

"STAR PLAYERS NEVER WIN ON THEIR OWN."

Teams will always have to make changes. It's a fact of competition and life that nothing goes to plan. The signifi-cance of developing a "next man/woman up" mindset from the beginning is missed by all but the very best coaches. Committing to such an approach means that all players must be treated fairly, or at least held to the same standards on and off the field.

Next, there is the issue of player development. All teams plan for succession after their current crop of stars retire or are traded, but good ones root this plan in coaching their bench players hard, if not harder than the first team. By coaching, I actually mean identifying limiting factors and mitigating them – what's the aspect of the game that is holding a player back from reaching their true potential and how can we remedy this?

This increases the standard and demands of play in practice, which in turn elevates the performance of the starters. Afterall, nobody knows a player or unit's tendencies or how to exploit their weakness better than their teammates. This approach also improves the overall coaching level and builds a natural succession plan.

Brian Smith (the brother of Tony Smith, who, if you may remember, went on to great success after losing the first 15 games of his career) has coached against Wayne Bennett's sides for years and they have always been fierce rivals. Tony learned a system of assessment from Brian that he used with all his players. Brian had a very analytical style that gave every player a score and ranking for game evaluation based not only on how well the individual themselves performed, but taking into account how they impacted the team's overall performance. This flies in the face of the current "me-first" trend of individual player stats being king in sports analytics.

Similarly, Jim Harbaugh would rank the entire squad from 1 to 135 each week. This kept players competitive through extrinsic motivation. He learned the importance of fostering continually fierce competition from Bo Schembechler and recognized that a line needed to be drawn between those who were driven to excel and the ones who didn't want it badly enough. Other coaches like Tony McGahan, Declan Kidney, and Brendan Rodgers use different approaches that foster an internal desire for improvement.

But development is not restricted to players alone. Backroom teams and support staff have become much bigger in the past few years. Though teams continue to spend the big bucks on filling their backrooms with experts, this investment rarely yields a proportional return in performance improvement. Instead of hiring every kind of guru they can think of, the smarter teams utilize consultants and third-party advisors thoughtfully.

How do you help your staff grow, and are you developing all of them or just the key people?

COROLLARY

Loyalty to players and staff creates loyalty from both in return. A sustained and cohesive system of play is established and maintained. But if players or staff are not up to a standard or cannot improve, they must be replaced.

APPLICATION

Establish development pathways for your players and staff. Assist them in identifying their aims and goals and then help them find a path to reach these. Doing so keeps your succession plan in clear view.

"You've got to
be yourself,
and if you're
not, you're
a phony. It
comes shining
through if
you're not
careful."

— JACK HARBAUGH

GET COMFORTABLE BEING UNCOMFORTABLE

59

Thrive on chaos and learn to accept the things you can't control.

I was sitting upstairs in the cafeteria at the Ospreys rugby facility. As the best regional side in Welsh rugby at that time, they had over 15 players on the Welsh national team. I would attend practice as often as I could to help, observe, and keep the channels of communication open. You can text and email all day, but most people, particularly Celtic people, appreciate you taking the effort to meet face to face.

Practice had ended for the day and players dragged their weary bodies up for some much-needed post-practice food. In rugby there is an unwritten rule: players eat first. Coaches and staff wait until afterwards and even if you're in line to eat and a player comes late, you stand back and let him move in front of you. Needless to say, I stayed by the window out of the way to wait.

As was standard for me, I sat quietly, scribbling random notes and thoughts in my ever-present small black notebook, which was so over-used it was falling apart at the spiral. Training had ended a while ago, and the players were flooding in to eat. But despite the rising clamor of their conversations, I still heard another noise outside and glanced over my shoulder. Down on the practice field, some people were still out on the grass. All wore coaching tracksuits except for one. A player was still in a jersey and shorts practicing drop goals (kicking the ball from distance between the sticks, if you're not a rugby fan).

Jerry Collins had just joined the Ospreys a few months before from the French club Toulon. A former All Black with almost 50 caps for the greatest rugby team ever to play the game, this was no ordinary player. Jerry was a legend. In Wales he was still remembered for a completely legal, but brutally forceful tackle in a World Cup game. Colin Charvis, then one of Wales's biggest players, was knocked out cold when Jerry met him with full force. As one commentator described it, Colin was knocked out from the legs up and unconscious before he hit the grass. Every rugby fan has a Jerry Collins memory. The only image more indelible than his ferocious tackles was his huge smile and blonde "Guinness" hairstyle.

But here after a long training session, was Jerry outside practicing things he might never be called on to use in a game. He ran, passed, kicked and worked relentlessly on his skills. As well as staying late, Jerry turned up for early morning work with youth team and skill position players even though he wasn't one. He truly loved the game.

"EMBRACE THE CHAOS."

It slowly dawned on me why Jerry was described by the coaches as one of the most adaptable players they had known. He trained for it. Jerry had such a passion for rugby that he was never simply happy knowing his own role and excelling in it. He wanted to be able to play anywhere. Watching him week in and week out, I started to see that his work-rate and seemingly limitless energy in games was no surprise. He always wanted to do more. He could adapt to the chaos of the game because he practiced for it. Every game he played he worked on something new.

Jerry told me that he'd once learned an important lesson from Keith Wood, the great Irish rugby player. Keith said that after something goes wrong or you make a mistake, you have to do two simple things: chop wood and carry water. This isn't meant in the literal sense, but rather infers that you need to stick with the basic habits and routines that made you successful in the first place. The other part of this is that you should engage in purposeful action to overcome a setback. Return to something you've mastered over the years to give yourself command of the situation, particularly when events start to feel like they're spiraling out of control. For me, that means going for a run or coaching someone. Do those simple things that you know you can do well, and you'll feel a lot better, even when the press turns on you and you're the subject of speculation and negative media coverage.

Jerry Collins and his partner, Alana Madill, tragically died in a car crash in the South of France in 2015. He was only 34. Jerry and Alana's three-month-old daughter survived. Even to this day, many people who played with and coached him can't bring themselves to talk about Jerry, such was the impact he had on them.

At the end of practice one day as I collected GPS units from the Welsh players we were tracking, Collins approached me and said, "You're Irish, what are you doing tracking these Welsh guys, bro?"

I turned around to see his big smile and sweat dripping down his face.

"No point tracking me," he said. "Those satellites aren't good enough for me."

You're right, Jerry. No one was.

Is your team excited and enthusiastic about the constant uncertainty they face?

COROLLARY

We are creatures who crave order. We find comfort from structure and patterns, which allow us to recover and regenerate. Such comforts are necessary in life. Days off and social events help reload and rebuild. But we make true progress amidst chaos and challenges.

APPLICATION

Embrace the uncomfortable. Life is not meant to be constantly straight or plain sailing. Find solace in knowing this and stay ready. In business and sports, prepare for inevitable chaos, randomness, and chance by anticipating and training for it.

"People learn in different ways, by studying the brain you learn why corrections work in some athletes, and not on others."

— HENK KRAAIJENHOF

THE FINAL LESSON

Throughout my career I have learned some remarkable lessons. But sometimes life itself teaches you lessons you don't see coming. As I finished this book, I experienced that first hand.

> "The truth is like a lion; you don't have to defend it.
> Let it loose; it will defend itself."
> —St. Augustine

I was combining two roles for the University of Michigan Football program, Performance Director (responsible for the performance, strength and conditioning, sports science, nutrition, player welfare) and Director of Operations (overseeing all areas of operation of the team functioning, events, meal planning, travel, hotels, flights, etc.). Either of these jobs alone is very demanding. Doing both invariably means working 14/16+ hour days, 7 days a week, year-round, especially if you take pride in being best-in-class in your work.

After two years non-stop, I finally took four days off to go back to home to see my family. Boarding the plane, I got a call from a friend at work. Without telling me, the director of player personnel had brought in someone to the head coach to interview for one of my jobs, director of operations. Shortly after I returned, sure enough, without notice, the role of director of operations was advertised online.

I was scheduled to travel to Tampa to speak to a donor group for a University fundraising event. Before I left for Tampa, I met with the athletic director to discuss a role we had discussed previously, providing sports science, health and welfare support to all student athletes. This was a role donors had offered funding for, and regents had supported. The athletic director promised to review the proposal and we'd connect after the Tampa trip.

However, 30 minutes after the meeting, I got a text from his assistant, the associate athletic director for football:

"[AD] asked me to reach out as he is in meetings until 4. Football has a new nutritionist starting Monday. Could you pack up over the weekend and we will have a new office for you when you get back from Florida? The ones in Weidenbach are already going to be occupied. He said you can give him a ring after four if you want to talk."

Naturally surprised, I went to the office, packed up and flew to Tampa a few days later. I returned from Tampa and waited to hear where my new office was going be and the new assignment. Days passed, without hearing anything from the head coach, athletic director or anyone. Slowly days turned into weeks. Going from long busy days, sur-rounded by the energy of players and coaches, to suddenly sitting at home each day, left me without a role or purpose. Coming off a steady diet of 16-hour days, this sudden inac-tivity was a shock to the system. Confused, trying to pro-tect friends and family and not wanting them to worry, I didn't reach out to share my concerns.

Everyone reading this goes through tough times. I've certainly had my share and I'd always been able to endure. But by the time I got to the fourth week, not being able to get an answer or hearing from the athletic director I grew more concerned about what was really going on and the true motives. Even though I was struggling to switch my mind off or sleep I was scared to take any sleeping medication. Eventually I wasn't sleeping at all. It was here that I made the mistake of turning to alcohol to try to switch off and fall asleep. While that alone is a mistake, driving the next morning was a bigger one. I crashed my car, was arrested and charged with DUI.

I've learned many lessons on and off the field, but this was certainly the most difficult. I had put my concern for others before myself for too long and not looked after my own health nor reached out for help when I should have. Not only had I let myself down, but also family and friends. The negative media attention following my arrest was unrelenting, and from my perspective, incomplete, which only added to my frustration. I was disappointed in myself and annoyed that no one understood the background or context.

When we make mistakes, we have two choices: stay there or my choice - pull yourself up, own your mistakes, and find a way back on the road to a healthy life. Luckily, I had help. They say, 'a friend loves at all times, and a brother is born for a time of adversity.' In the days that followed I found out I had some really special brothers (and sisters) who stepped up in my time of adversity.

My phone started ringing almost constantly from players, friends, university donors, former coaches, players and colleagues from around the world, who knowing me offering to help. Friends from the special operations community who reached out helped me most of all, sharing their private experiences helping me keep perspective and move on. This was a truly humbling experience. Almost every single person shared a story of something they had overcome. It dawned on me that I was not unique, what was perhaps different was that mine made the news. It also taught me first that there is often more to any story we read. One thing is guaranteed in life - everyone makes mistakes. Some never learn or even regress, but success is about learning from failures and becoming even better. When life comes at you fast, heed this lesson most of all.

Will this happen to you? And when, how do you overcome it?

COROLLARY

We all need to work hard for periods, but are you putting physical and psychological health below that of other priorities? Are you sacrificing family time for something that is really not that important? Are you sacrificing sleep, friendships, social life and of course, health?

APPLICATION

There is always positives that come from any traumatic event. Learn the lesson. Don't over extend. Keep your priorities straight. I visited St. Frances Academy in Baltimore and surrounded by homeless kids who had literally nothing, kept in perspective. People you thought were friends aren't there for you, good. Those are who are, are your true friends. Start your next project. I wrote two books and started another. I started my consultancy business, mentoring corporate leaders, performance directors, coaches, and special operations groups, something I've always wanted to. Find the positives.

CONCLUSION

When mentoring performance directors, business executives or speaking corporate groups I am asked for the best advice I can give them to be successful in their fields.

Never, ever quit. Almost every truly great player I've worked with told me they were written off, cut from a team, or constantly criticized. Most said something to the effect of, "I wasn't that good when I was younger," or "My older brother/sister was actually way better than I was,". Never, ever, ever quit. Make someone else stop you, but never stop yourself.

Commit completely. We're not saving lives here, but what we're doing is still important and impactful: developing young people for life through sports. First, do no harm. Look after the players and staff under your care and build lasting relationships with them. The best piece of advice I got after I messed up years ago was, "The person who never made a mistake, never made anything."

Never run from a problem. It's a learning experience. Be Loyal. Never bully, intimidate, or attack anyone. But at the same time, never allow it to happen to you. Always stand your ground. Have moral courage. Allow yourself to be vulnerable and learn from it, but don't suffer weakness. You will be brought to your knees occasionally, but you cannot roll on your back.

Say it as you see it. Sure, at times you'll make people uncomfortable. But those who accept your blunt, objective view will become real friends for life and you'll get to the heart of every matter faster. Remember that in training, coaching, and life, the truth is what you should keep searching for.

Stay humble. To continually improve requires remaining honest with yourself, no matter what the circumstances. Being brave doesn't mean being stupid. You have to face reality and facts. Don't fool yourself – there will be plenty of people eager to do that for you. Be brutally honest with the person staring back at you in the mirror. And stay humble, regardless of what worldly achievements you accumulate. Humility brings self-awareness, which in turn results in faster learning outcomes.

Ask. More people will help you than you know, if you're willing to ask for assistance. On the other side of the equation, many of the folks I've worked with continue to call me for advice on various aspects of management, coaching, and life. As a rule, we are probably one of the most obliging professions - when asked for help. Get a mentor, listen carefully to them, and put their tutelage into practice. Then pass it on.

Enjoy the journey and laugh! A smile and humor is the best way to break the ice in just about every setting. Having worked in many countries, I've seen that even when you have little or nothing in common with the people you work with, introducing humor is the fastest and easiest way to start a relationship.

EPILOGUE

In 2005, I sent an email to a chiropractor named Mike Prebeg who works in Toronto with professional athletes. I reached out to him because although I was accepted to medical school at the Royal College of Surgeons in Dublin, I was considering studying at McMaster University in Toronto instead. I'm pretty sure Mike does not remember either getting or replying to the email since it was so long ago.

But to this day, I've never forgotten the first line of his reply:

"I have had many great opportunities and influential people help me along the way and would love to help anyone else that is interested."

Mentoring and helping good people do great things is truly my passion and the motivation behind sharing the lessons in this book.

And that's really what this book comes down to – learning from the best so you can be *your* best.

SHOULDERS OF GIANTS

Over the years, I've been fortunate to stand on the shoulders of so many giants, coaches, and players. Most are mentioned here and some I've not been able to name. Malcolm X's quote bears repeating: "Only the mistakes have been mine."

I'm eternally grateful for the friendship, help, and support so many people have shown me over the years. Everything I know I've learned directly from people referenced in this book. This is my way to thank them and to pass on and share their wisdom with the next generation of young coaches.

I'm also deeply thankful for everyone.

My family has always been unconditionally supportive.

Special thanks to Biff & Amy Poggi, Katie Fraumann, Jim & Heidi Minick, Nate Barry, Zach Eisendrath, Andrea Fischer Newman, Dan Pfaff, Jorge Carvajal, Anthony Donskov, Tim Smith, Mark Naylor, Justin Smith, Cameron & Jen Josse, Joe Simon, Victoria You, Will Tishkoff Kimberley Hoskins, Kacey O'Neill, Brooke Mathis, Chris Vukelich, ██████████, Houston Hoskins, Matthew ███████████, Mark Bennett, Conleith Gilligan, Gerrit Keferstein, Tom ███████████, Brett Bartholomew, Brendan Fanning, Angus Reid, Alan McConnell, Bryan Mann, Yosef Johnson, Bryan Doo, John Weatherly, Larry Sanders, Ron McKeefry, Todd Hamer, Patrick ███████████, Teena Murray, Verena & Henk Kraaijenhof, Joe ███████, Amber & Jedd Fisch, Riley Ross, Phil Johnson, Ian McMahon, Phil White, Alex ███████████, Tim Drevno, Ashley Jones, Phil Richards, Eric Mangini,

David McCague, Mike ████████, James Conlon, Tom Moyna, Seamus Mullen, Sal Alosi, Ron Lynn, Ben Clerkin, Martin Kennedy, Craig White, Kelly Tatarelli-Mullins, Stu McMillan, John ████████, Phil White, Mike Boyle, Rick Finotti, Jason Williams, Whitney Tarver, Mick McDermott, Chris Borland, Mike Hughes, DeAnna McDaniels, Henry Barrera, Paul Kimmage, Steve Moser, Tom Myslinski, AJ Neibel, Ron Lynn, David Piche, Charlie Jenks, Milot Goci, Tom Gamble, Don Brown, Justin Bokmeyer, James Smith, Mike ████████, Art Horne, Alan O'Connell, ████████, ████████, and many, many more. To all my Welsh, Niners, Wales, Liverpool and Michigan players and many others thank you all. Chris Jones, Dennis Tice, Mike Tice, and Chris Rosenthal, who I still believe I owe rent to for spending days on end finishing this book at Tobacco Rose, his cigar shop in Ann Arbor.

There are many others who I can't name for obvious reasons, but you know I never forget.

To you all, "Thank you," is simply not enough.

THE TEACHERS

SAMUEL ALLARDYCE is an English football manager and former professional player, who left his post as manager at Premier League club Everton in May 2018. As a player, Allardyce made 578 league and cup appearances in a 21-year career. Allardyce made his managerial debut in the Premier League with Bolton Wanderers, where he spent much of his playing career. The Englishman also represented Millwall, Coventry City, Preston North End, and Sunderland between 1980-81.

BILL BELICHICK is the head coach of the New England Patriots of the National Football League (NFL). Belichick, also general manager of the team, is regarded as one of the most successful coaches in any sport. He holds many records, including winning five Super Bowls.

WAYNE BENNETT is an Australian professional rugby league coach and former player. He is the head coach of the Brisbane Broncos in the NRL, and since 2016 he has also been head coach of the England national team, the first non-English coach to hold the position. He was also head coach of Australia in 1998 and from 2004 to 2005, and was an assistant coach of New Zealand in 2008. Widely regarded as one of the sport's greatest ever coaches, he holds Australian coaching records for most grand final wins and most seasons with a single club (24 with the Broncos).

ANQUAN BOLDIN is a former American football wide receiver who spent 14 seasons in the National Football League (NFL). He played college football at Florida State and was drafted by the Arizona Cardinals in the second round of the 2003 NFL draft. He also played for the Baltimore Ravens, San Francisco 49ers, and Detroit Lions. Boldin was the 2003 NFL Offensive Rookie of the Year, was selected to three Pro Bowls and won Super Bowl XLVII with the Ravens. In 2015, he was named the Walter Payton Man of the Year for his community service.

CHRIS BORLAND is a former American football linebacker who played for the San Francisco 49ers. He played college football at Wisconsin and was drafted by the 49ers in the third round of the 2014 NFL Draft. He is one of the first NFL players to retire from professional football early in his career due to concerns over head injuries inherent to the sport. In an outstanding rookie season with the 49ers, he won defensive player of the week twice.

NAVORRO RODERICK BOWMAN is an American football linebacker who played for the San Francisco 49ers and Oakland Raiders in the NFL. He played college football at Penn State, and was drafted by the 49ers in the third round of the 2010 NFL Draft. Selected for the Pro Bowl three times, he was one of the most dominant linebackers of the past decade.

NATHAN BUCKLEY is an Australian rules football coach and former professional player, best known for his time as captain of the Collingwood Football Club in the Australian Football League (AFL). He is currently Collingwood's senior coach.

GREGORY CHAPPELL MBE is a former cricketer who represented Australia at international level in both Tests and One-Day Internationals (ODIs). The second of three brothers to play Test cricket, Chappell was the pre-eminent Australian batsman of his time who had both an elegant stroke and fierce concentration. An exceptional all-round player who bowled medium pace and, at his retirement, held the world record for the most catches in Test cricket, Chappell's career straddled two eras as the game moved toward a greater level of professionalism.

ALASTAIR CLARKSON is an Australian rules football coach and former player. He has been the head coach of the Hawthorn Football Club in the Australian Football League (AFL) since 2004 and is the longest-serving coach in the league.

THE CLEVELAND BROWNS is a professional American football team based in Cleveland, Ohio. The Browns compete in the National Football League (NFL) as a member club of the American Football Conference (AFC) North division. They play their home games at FirstEnergy Stadium, which opened in 1999, with administrative offices and training facilities in Berea, Ohio. The Browns' official colors are brown, orange, and white. They are unique among the 32 member franchises of the NFL in that they do not have a logo on their helmets.

VICTOR CONTE is a former bassist with the band Tower of Power and the founder and president of Bay Area Laboratory Co-operative (BALCO), a sports nutrition center in California. He served time in prison in 2005 after pleading guilty to conspiracy to distribute steroids and money laundering. Conte played a role in tarnishing professional sports with his distribution of illegal performance enhancing drugs. He currently operates Scientific Nutrition for Advanced Conditioning (SNAC Nutrition).

TOM CREAN is an American college basketball coach and the current head coach for the Georgia Bulldogs. Crean was previously the head coach of the Indiana Hoosiers men's basketball team. Prior to that, he served as head coach at Marquette University (1999–2008), where the program averaged 20 wins a year and made six postseason appearances, including the 2003 NCAA Final Four.

CRICKET AUSTRALIA (CA), formerly known as the Australian Cricket Board (ACB), is the governing body for professional and amateur cricket in Australia. It was originally formed in 1905 as the "Australian Board of Control for International Cricket." CA operates all of the Australian national representative cricket sides, including the Australian men's cricket team, the women's national cricket team, and youth sides as well. CA is also responsible for organizing and hosting Test tours and One-Day Internationals with other nations and scheduling the home international fixtures.

SIR KENNY DALGLISH is a Scottish former football player and manager. He made over three hundred appearances for both Celtic and Liverpool and earned over one hundred caps for the Scotland national team. Dalglish won the Ballon d'Or Silver Award in 1983, the PFA Players' Player of the Year in 1983, and the FWA Footballer of the Year in

1979 and 1983. Dalglish was the first player to score 100 goals in both Scottish and English soccer. Named player-manager late in his career with Liverpool, he went on to managerial and executive roles with Blackburn, Newcastle United, and Celtic.

VERNON DAVIS is an American football tight end for the Washington Redskins in the NFL and played college football at Maryland. He was drafted by the San Francisco 49ers sixth overall in the 2006 NFL Draft. In 2009, Davis co-led the NFL in touchdown receptions. In the 2011–12 NFL playoffs with the 49ers, Davis caught the game-winning touchdown pass from Alex Smith against the New Orleans Saints, referred to by fans and the media as "The Catch III." In 2015, Davis was traded to the Denver Broncos, with whom he won Super Bowl 50. The following season, he signed with the Washington Redskins.

BERNARD DUNNE is an Irish former professional boxer and a former WBA (Regular) world champion and European Super Bantamweight champion. He started his career under the legendary Freddie Roach at the Wild Card Boxing Club in Los Angeles. On Saturday, March 21, 2009, Dunne defeated Ricardo Cordoba in the 11th round to become the WBA (Regular) super bantamweight world champion in a fight that won ESPN's 2009 Fight of The Year, with six knockdowns occurring in the fight (four for Dunne and two for Cordoba). Dunne retired on February 19, 2010. He is currently the performance director for Irish Boxing.

SHAUN EDWARDS is a rugby union coach and former professional rugby league footballer. He is the assistant coach (defense) of Wales, a post he has held since 2008. A scrum-half or stand-off in rugby league, Edwards is the most decorated player in rugby league history, with 37 winners' medals. In 2015 he was the 25th person inducted into the Rugby League Hall of Fame. Edwards was capped 36 times for Great Britain and played for England in 1995 and 1996 and Ireland in 1998. In all, he appeared in three Rugby League World Cups.

VITOR FRADE is the creator of a football training methodology called Tactical Periodization. José Mourinho was a student of his at the University of Porto. Frade, who developed this model in the 1990s, is also a mentor to Rui Faria, André Villas-Boas, José Tavares, and Vítor Pereira. Frade has been a professor at the Faculty of Sport at the University of Porto for 35 years. He began as a coach, first in volleyball and then in professional football.

CHARLIE FRANCIS was an Olympic sprinter and sprint coach from Canada. He was the coach of sprinters Ben Johnson, Angella Issajenko, Mark McKoy, and Desai Williams. Francis was banned by Athletics Canada following his admissions at the 1989 Dublin Inquiry that he had introduced Johnson to steroids. He went on to coach and mentor coaches in many sports. He authored two books on sprinting: *Speed Trap* and *Training for Speed* and was the owner/operator of a popular internet sprint training forum.

WARREN GATLAND is a New Zealand rugby union coach and currently the head coach of Wales. Since he took over this role in 2007, Wales have won three Six Nations titles, including two Grand Slams, and reached the semi-final of the 2011 World Cup. Gatland was also head coach of the British and Irish Lions on their 2013 tour of Australia, where they won the Test series 2-1, and 2017 tour of New Zealand, when the series was a draw.

JIM GAVIN is the Gaelic football manager of the Dublin inter-county team and a former player. He has been the manager of the Dublin senior team since 2012, where he has since become one of the county's most successful managers. Raised in Clondalkin, South Dublin, he won three Leinster titles, one All-Ireland and one National Football League trophy as a player. He has also won five National Football League titles, five Leinster Titles, and four All-Ireland Titles as a manager. Gavin is regarded as one of the best minds in the modern game.

STEVEN GERRARD is an English professional football manager and former player, who is currently the manager of Scottish Premiership club Rangers. He spent the majority of his playing career as a central midfielder for Liverpool, with most of that time spent as club captain, as well as captaining the England national team. Regarded as one of the greatest midfielders of his generation, Gerrard was awarded the UEFA Club Footballer of the Year award in 2005, and the Ballon d'Or Bronze Award.

KELVIN GILES is a former UK National and Olympic Track & Field Coach. He is currently the CEO and founder of Movement Dynamics. Kelvin is the former director of performance at Brisbane Broncos, head coach at the Australian Institute of Sport, UK National T&F Coach, and one of the world's first performance directors.

FRANK GORE is an American football running back for the Miami Dolphins of the National Football League (NFL). He played college football for the University of Miami and was drafted by the San Francisco 49ers in the third round of the 2005 NFL Draft and starred for them from 2005 to 2014. He is the 49ers all-time leader in rushing yards and rushing touchdowns.

TONY GRANATO is an American former professional ice hockey left winger and current head coach of the Wisconsin Badgers men's ice hockey team. He also served as head coach of the United States men's national ice hockey team at the 2018 Winter Olympics. Previously, Tony was head coach of the National Hockey League (NHL)'s Colorado Avalanche, as well as being an assistant coach for the Detroit Red Wings and Pittsburgh Penguins.

THE GREATER WESTERN SYDNEY GIANTS, nicknamed the GWS Giants or just Giants, is a professional Australian rules football club which plays in the Australian Football League (AFL). Representing the Greater Western Sydney area and Canberra, the club is based at the Tom Wills Oval in Sydney Olympic Park. GWS's primary home ground is Spotless Stadium in Sydney Olympic Park. Four games a year are played at Manuka Oval in Canberra as part of a deal with the government of the Australian Capital Territory.

JACK HARBAUGH is a former American football player and coach. He is known for being the longtime head coach at Western Kentucky. Jack is also the father of the first pair of brothers to serve as NFL head coaches and also face off in a Super Bowl: John and Jim Harbaugh.

PÁDRAIG HARRINGTON is an Irish professional golfer who plays on the European Tour and the PGA Tour. He has won three major championships: The Open Championship in 2007 and 2008 and the PGA Championship, also in 2008. He has spent over 300 weeks in the top-10 of the Official World Golf Ranking and reached a career-high world ranking of third in July 2008.

NEIL JENKINS is a former rugby union player and current Wales national rugby union team kicking skills coach. He played fly-half, center, and full back for Pontypridd, Cardiff, Celtic Warriors, Wales, and the British and Irish Lions. Jenkins is Wales' highest ever points-scorer and is third highest on the list of leading rugby union Test point scorers. He was the first player to score 1,000 points in international matches.

CHARLIE JENKS is a retired US Army Colonel who now focuses on helping with their health and wellness, and also working with veterans to lead a more productive and healthy life. Charlie served in Afghanistan twice, which earned his awards for valor. He has an M.S. in Human Nutrition and an M.S. in Strategic Studies, and now lives in Santa Cruz, CA, where he runs fast-growing nutrition and martial arts businesses.

SCOTT JOHNSON is an Australian rugby union coach, who was the interim head coach for Scotland in 2013 and early 2014, and the current director of rugby for Scotland Rugby. Johnson played for Parramatta Two Blues and Eastwood and was captain of both the New South Wales Waratahs and Australian Under 21s. Johnson has coached Wales, the United States, Ospreys, and Scotland.

ASHLEY JONES has been a professional strength and conditioning coach for over 25 years across three sports: basketball, rugby league, and rugby union. He is currently the head of physical preparation for the Samoan Rugby Union based in Apia, Samoa. He previously worked with three other international rugby teams (New Zealand All Blacks, Australia, and Scotland) and professional clubs in New Zealand (Crusaders), Japan (Panasonic), and Scotland (Edinburgh). He was awarded the NSCA Professional Coach of the Year for 2016.

COLIN KAEPERNICK is an American football quarterback who is currently a free agent. Kaepernick played college football for the University of Nevada in Reno. After graduating, he was selected by the San Francisco 49ers in the second round of the 2011 NFL Draft. In 2016, after kneeling during the playing of the US national anthem prior to NFL games in protest to what he believed to be racial injustices against black Americans, Kaepernick pledged to donate one million dollars to "organizations working in oppressed communities." In 2017, Kaepernick was named GQ magazine's Citizen of the Year for his efforts and in April 2018, Amnesty International honored Kaepernick with the 2018 Ambassador of Conscience Award.

JOHN KAVANAGH is an Irish martial arts coach, Brazilian Jiu-Jitsu practitioner, and former professional mixed martial artist. His students include fighters such as Conor McGregor, Eden Payne, Bayley Dynan, and Gunnar Nelson. He is the founder and head coach of Irish MMA gym Straight Blast Gym Ireland and the current president of the Irish Mixed Martial Arts Association. Kavanagh is known as one of the best MMA coaches in the world, having been nominated for the World MMA Awards Coach of the Year in 2016 and winning it in 2017.

AMIR KHAN is a British professional boxer. He is a former unified light-welterweight world champion, having held the WBA (later Super) title from 2009 to 2012, and the IBF title in 2011. At a regional level, he held the Commonwealth lightweight title from 2007 to 2008. He also held the WBC Silver welterweight title from 2014 to 2016, and once challenged for a middleweight world title in 2016. As an amateur, Khan won a silver medal in the lightweight division at the 2004 Olympics, becoming, at the age of 17, Britain's youngest boxing Olympic medalist. He is a philanthropist with his own charity organization, Amir Khan Foundation.

PAUL KIMMAGE is an Irish sports journalist who, until his departure in early 2012, wrote for *The Sunday Times* newspaper in the United Kingdom. He is also a former professional road bicycle racer. Since writing *Rough Ride* about his time as a cyclist, Paul has gone on to become one of the world's most respected sports journalists. In January 2011, nyvelocity.com published the full transcript of a seven-hour interview with Floyd Landis, in which Landis admitted to being involved in doping activities during his time with the US Postal team. Kimmage wrote the award-winning biography of Matt Hampson, *Engage: The Fall and Rise of Matt Hampson*, published in August 2011.

LES KISS is an Australian former professional rugby league footballer who played in the New South Wales Rugby League and is now a coach. Kiss was appointed defensive coach with the Ireland national rugby union team under head coach Declan Kidney in 2009. He is currently head coach at London Irish having previously been assistant head coach of Ireland and director of rugby of Ulster.

BILL KNOWLES is a world-renowned expert in rehabilitation and reconditioning, having worked with athletes and teams from across the globe at the Olympic, world-class, and professional levels. Knowles is a certified/licensed athletic trainer (ATC/L-ATC) and a certified strength and conditioning specialist (CSCS) with over 25 years of experience at the world-class, professional, Olympic, and elite youth levels. Bill graduated from the State University of New York College at Cortland in 1989 with a degree in Athletic Training/Sports Medicine.

HENK KRAAIJENHOF has worked with elite athletes in many sports. He now serves as an international performance consultant in a wide range of fields, including for corporations, organizations, military, and police departments. Henk is an international lecturer in these fields and the author of three books. He has coached Nelli Cooman, Merlene Ottey, Troy Douglas, and tennis star Mary Pierce. Henk is a world renowned expert in physical and mental coaching.

IVAN LENDL is a former Czech-American professional tennis player. He is often considered among the greatest in the sport's history. He was the world No. 1 for 270 weeks in the 1980s and finished his career with 94 singles titles. At the majors he won eight Grand Slam titles and was runner-up a record 11 times. He also won seven year-end championships.

As a tennis coach, he has helped Andy Murray win three major titles and reach the world No. 1 ranking.

LIVERPOOL FOOTBALL CLUB is a professional soccer club in Liverpool, England, that competes in the Premier League. The club has won five European Cups, three UEFA Cups, three UEFA Super Cups, 18 League titles, seven FA Cups, eight League Cups, and 15 FA Community Shields. Founded in 1892, Liverpool joined the Football League the following year and has played at Anfield since its formation. Liverpool established itself as a major force in English and European football in the 1970s and 1980s when Bill Shankly and Bob Paisley led the club to 11 League titles and seven European trophies.

MICHAEL MALTHOUSE is a former Australian rules footballer and former Australian Football League (AFL) coach and current media personality. His playing career included a premiership for Richmond in 1980. He is best known for his long coaching career at four clubs and holds the record for coaching the most VFL/AFL games.

RAY MCDONALD is a former American football defensive end who played for the San Francisco 49ers and Chicago Bears. He was drafted by the 49ers in the third round of the 2007 NFL Draft. He played college football at Florida, where he was a member of a BCS National Championship team.

MUNSTER RUGBY is one of the four professional provincial rugby teams in Ireland. They compete in the Pro14 and the European Rugby Champions Cup. The team represents the IRFU Munster Branch, which is responsible for rugby union throughout the geographical Irish province of Munster. Their main home ground is Thomond Park. The team motto is, "To the brave and faithful, nothing is impossible."

TOM MYSLINSKI is a professional American football strength and conditioning coach for the Jacksonville Jaguars. He was strength and conditioning coach for the Cleveland Browns until the end of the 2009 season. Tom is also a former National Football League offensive lineman. He was originally drafted by the Dallas Cowboys in the 1992 NFL Draft and played nine seasons in the NFL for seven different teams.

NEW YORK KNICKS, commonly referred to as the Knicks, are an American professional basketball team based in the borough of Manhattan, in New York City. The Knicks compete in the National Basketball Association (NBA) as a member of the Atlantic Division of the Eastern Conference. The team plays its home games at Madison Square Garden.

DONNCHA O'CALLAGHAN is a retired Irish rugby union player. He began his career with his home province Munster, spending 17 seasons with the province and winning five major trophies, before finishing his career with Worcester Warriors in the English Premiership. Internationally, O'Callaghan represented Ireland and was part of the team that won the Six Nations grand slam in 2009. He also toured with the British and Irish Lions in 2005 and 2009, winning four caps, and was invited to play for the Barbarians twice.

PAUL O'CONNELL is a retired Irish rugby union player. He is Ireland's third most-capped player (108) and the eighteenth most-capped international player in rugby union history. During his career, O'Connell captained Munster, Ireland, and the British and Irish Lions. He is regarded as Ireland's greatest ever rugby player. Paul is currently an assistant coach with the Ireland under-20s rugby team.

MICK O'DWYER is a former Gaelic football manager and player. Mick is regarded as the greatest manager in the history of the game. He most famously managed the Kerry senior team between 1974 and 1989, during which time he became the county's longest-serving manager and most successful in terms of major titles won.

STEVE PETERS is an English psychiatrist who works in elite sports. Steve has clients across a wide range of disciplines, from health and education to business and elite sports, and he also works with members of the public. He is best known for his work with British Cycling. Steve currently competes in the M60 age group in master's athletics and is a multiple world champion.

DAN PFAFF is a track and field (athletics) coach, who has coached national, world, and Olympic championship athletes. Pfaff has worked with the likes of Donovan Bailey, Bruny Surin, and Glenroy Gilbert, as well as Greg Rutherford, who won the London 2012 Olympics in the men's long jump. Dan has managed both the United States Olympic Training Center and Lee Valley Athletics Centre for United Kingdom Athletics (UKA), to organize the coaching and training of the UK's athletes in the run-up to the 2012 London Olympics. Pfaff is currently one of the coaches at the ALTIS Performance Group in Phoenix, Arizona.

FRANCIS "BIFF" POGGI, was the head coach at Gilman High School, Baltimore for 19 years. A former Gilman football player, Poggi led the Greyhounds to 13 Maryland Interscholastic Athletic Association A Conference championships. He was associate head coach at the University of Michigan in 2016 and is the current head coach at St. Frances Academy in Baltimore, the number one ranked high school team in the USA.

CHARLES POLIQUIN was a Canadian strength coach and author of eight books on strength and conditioning. He earned a master's degree in Exercise Physiology and has published articles in peer-reviewed journals of exercise science and strength and conditioning. In the late 1990s, Poliquin founded Poliquin Performance and opened the first Poliquin Performance Center in Phoenix, Arizona in 2001. He has trained numerous Olympic and professional athletes.

CARLOS QUEIROZ is a Portuguese soccer coach currently in charge of the Iranian national team. He has also been the manager of the Portugal national team and Spanish club Real Madrid, and was Alex Ferguson's assistant manager at English club Manchester United. Queiroz has qualified three national teams for the World Cup: South Africa in 2002, Portugal in 2010, and Iran in 2014 and 2018.

DAVID RATH is the coaching development manager for the AFL (Australian Football League). He served as high-performance coach for the Hawthorn Hawks AFL for 13 years. Rath was Hawthorn coach Alastair Clarkson's first hire after he took over in late 2004. Rath was also a biomechanist and performance analyst at Australian Institute of Sport.

ERIC REID is an American football strong safety who is currently a free agent. He played college football for Louisiana State University (LSU), and received consensus All-American recognition. Eric was selected by the San Francisco 49ers in the first round of the 2013 NFL Draft. A standout track and field athlete as well, Reid was a Pro Bowl selection in 2013.

THE SAN FRANCISCO 49ERS are a professional American football team located in the San Francisco Bay Area. They compete in the National Football League (NFL) as a member of the league's National Football Conference (NFC) West division. The team currently plays its home games at Levi's Stadium in Santa Clara, California. The San Francisco 49ers have won five Super Bowl championships and six Conference Championships.

RICHARD SBRAGIA is a Scottish football coach and former player who is currently the manager of Manchester United Under-23s. His playing career saw him represent Birmingham City, Walsall, Blackpool, York City, and Darlington. Richard had a brief spell in his homeland when Birmingham loaned him to Morton. He has had an extensive coaching career, having coached at Manchester United, Bolton, and Sunderland, where he was briefly the manager.

JOE SCHMIDT is a New Zealand-born Irish rugby union coach, who is currently the head coach of Ireland. During his tenure, Ireland has won three Six Nations Championships in five years under his leadership. Joe's first head coaching role in Europe was with Leinster Rugby, beginning in 2010. He brought unprecedented success to the province, reaching six finals and winning four trophies in three years. Joe was previously an assistant coach with the Blues and Clermont Auvergne.

LOUIE SIMMONS is an American powerlifter and strength coach. He is noted for developing the Westside Barbell method of training and applying it to powerlifting and other sports, and inventing several widely used pieces of strength training equipment. Westside Barbell is his elite, private, invitation-only facility in Columbus, Ohio. Louie is one of only five lifters to total Elite in five different powerlifting weight classes and across various power-lifting organizations.

JUSTIN "COWBOY" SMITH is a former American football defensive end who played in the National Football League (NFL) for 13 years. He played college football at Missouri, where he was an All-American, and was drafted by the Cincinnati Bengals fourth overall in the 2001 NFL Draft. Smith played for the San Francisco 49ers and is recognized as one of the greatest defensive ends ever to play the game.

TONY SMITH is a professional rugby league coach and former player. He has coached Super League clubs Huddersfield Giants, Leeds Rhinos, and Warrington Wolves, as well as the England national rugby league team. He is the younger brother of fellow rugby league coach Brian Smith and uncle to former Tongan national team coach, Rohan Smith.

███████████████████████████████████████. The unit undertakes a number of roles including covert reconnaissance, counterterrorism, direct action, and hostage rescue.

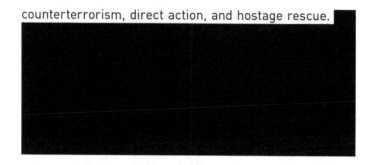

DR. KELLY STARRETT is the author of the *The New York Times* bestsellers *Becoming A Supple Leopard* and *Ready to Run*, the *Wall Street Journal* bestseller, *Deskbound*, and the acclaimed *Waterman 2.0*, all of which have revolutionized how coaches, athletes, and everyday humans approach performance as it relates to movement, mechanics, and the actualization of athletic potential. Kelly is also the co-founder of San Francisco CrossFit and MobilityWOD. com, where he shares his innovative approach to movement, mechanics, and mobility with millions of coaches and athletes around the world.

BILL SWEETENHAM is one of the world's most successful elite swimming coaches. He has coached the Australian, British, Hong Kong, and Argentinian national swimming teams. During his career, Sweetenham was head national team coach at five Olympic Games, coached 27 medalists at the Olympics and World Championships, and worked with nine world record holders.

range of tactical areas, including unconventional warfare, direct action, counterterrorism, special reconnaissance, and personnel recovery.

KEENA TURNER is an American football executive and former player, coach, and broadcaster. He was selected by the Miami Dolphins in the second round of the 1980 NFL Draft and traded on draft day to the San Francisco 49ers. A 6′2″ 237-pound linebacker from Purdue University, Keena played in 11 NFL seasons, spent his entire career with the 49ers. A one-time Pro Bowl selection, he retired from the 49ers with four Super Bowl rings.

TANA UMAGA is a former New Zealand rugby union player and former captain of the national team, the All Blacks. Since 2016 he has been coach of the Blues in the Super Rugby competition. He played for the Hurricanes from Super 12's inception in 1996 and took over the captaincy in 2003. Graham Henry named Tana as All Blacks captain in 2004 and under his leadership, the All Blacks won 19 of their 21 games, including the clean sweep of the British and Irish Lions and the Grand Slam in 2005. At the end of 2005, after 74 Test caps (where he scored 36 tries), Tana retired from international rugby.

CHARLES VAN COMMENEE is a Dutch athletics coach. He began his professional career as a technical director with the Dutch athletics federation before moving to take up a similar role for the British athletics team in 2001. After a term as performance director for the Dutch Olympic Committee, he served as head coach of British Athletics from 2008 to 2012. Additionally, he has personally coached athletes to international medals, including Denise Lewis, Kelly Sotherton, and Huang Zhihong.

CRAIG WHITE is a high-performance coach who has spent 25 years working in Rugby Union at every level. Craig has worked for teams such as Ireland, Wales, British and Irish Lions, London Wasps, and Leicester Tigers. He has also been a consultant to World Rugby (the sport's governing body) over the last six years, a role that has taken him all across the world to support developing rugby nations.

PATRICK WILLIS is a former American football linebacker who played his entire eight-year career with the San Francisco 49ers in the NFL. He was drafted by the 49ers in the first round of the 2007 NFL Draft. Patrick played college football for the University of Mississippi and received consensus All-American honors. He was a seven-time Pro Bowler and is regarded as one of the greatest linebackers in the modern game.

SIR CLIVE WOODWARD OBE is a former English rugby union player and coach. He was coach of the England team from 1997 to 2004, managing them to victory in the 2003 Rugby World Cup. From 2000 to 2003, England won 41 of their 46 matches, including a perfect record of 20-0 at Twickenham and 12 successive wins against the Tri Nations. As part of this stretch, Woodward led England to winning the inaugural Six Nations, and a Grand Slam title.

███████████ foreign internal defense, special reconnaissance, direct action, and counterterrorism.

FERGUS

Fergus Connolly is one of the world's leading experts in team sports and human performance. He is the only coach to have worked full-time in every major league around the world. Fergus helps teams win at the highest level with the integrated application of best practices in all areas of performance. His highly acclaimed book *Game Changer* (with Phil White) is the first blueprint for coaches to present a holistic philosophy for winning in all team sports.

Fergus has served as director of elite performance for the San Francisco 49ers, sports science director with the Welsh Rugby Union, and performance director and director of football operations for University of Michigan Football. He has mentored and advised coaches, support staff, and players in the NBA, MLB, NHL, Australian Rules Football, and international cricket. Fergus has also trained world boxing champions and advises elite military units and companies across the globe.

He is a keynote speaker and consultant to high performing organizations around the world.

Learn more at
http://www.fergusconnolly.com

CPSIA information can be obtained
at www.ICGtesting.com
Printed in the USA
LVHW021500120721
692484LV00012B/939